T0248072

Advance Praise for
JUSTIFY THIS

"The one-and-only Nick Searcy tells his story in the way only he can. His honesty, patriotism, and love of truth make this a readable and inspiring book."

—*Dinesh D'Souza,* bestselling author
and political commentator

"Nick Searcy is nobody's bitch. Like the hard-bitten characters he portrays, this guy plays by his own rules in a world he never made. For the based, *Justify This* is great reading. For low-T sissies, it's a much-needed injection of Vitamin Manhood."

—*Kurt Schlichter,* author and pundit

"I always wanted to read more about Nick Searcy to see if he's as cool as he always says he is. Well, it's now confirmed in print by, guess who? That's right, Nick himself, in *Justify This*. Throughout his amazing career, my friend Nick has fearlessly voiced his conservative beliefs in an industry openly hostile to those beliefs. Way easier said than done. For that alone he deserves our grateful support. Get this great book."

—*David Limbaugh,* author

Praise for
NICK SEARCY

"Nick Searcy is so much more than a *delightful* actor, he's also the most *wonderful* pro wrestling manager I've ever had!"
—*Matt Hardy,* professional wrestler

"I wish everybody could meet Nick Searcy. He's an actor, he's an accomplished actor, movies, television shows, and you'd love to hang around him, watch a ball game, have a beer, chew the fat. Just a great guy. He's totally fearless. I mean, you can count 'em on one hand, fearless Hollywood conservatives. He does not hide it, doesn't use it as an excuse. I don't think he trumpets it, but he doesn't hide it. Well, not true to say he doesn't trumpet it. I mean, he's very proud of it."
—*Rush Limbaugh,* The Rush Limbaugh Show, Feb. 6, 2014

"Aside from his amazing talent as an actor, director and producer—and yes, even a radio broadcaster—Nick Searcy exemplifies American exceptionalism in his unflinching defense of the American Dream. He is a treasure to our nation and to humanity."
—*James Golden/Bo Snerdley,* The Rush Limbaugh Show

"Nick Searcy is an American treasure. Like Ronald Reagan, he is more than an actor. He is a leader. He follows his conscience, fearlessly. He is a patriot. He's built of sterner stuff."
—*Michael Berry,* radio host

"Nick Searcy doesn't wear a cape, but he's a hero to me."
—*Dean Cain,* Superman/Clark Kent in Lois & Clark: The New Adventures of Superman

"I know Nick Searcy."
—*Jeremy Boreing,* cofounder of The Daily Wire

JUSTIFY THIS

A CAREER WITHOUT
COMPROMISE

NICK SEARCY

WITH JOHNNY RUSSO

FOREWORDS BY LARRY CORREIA AND GRAHAM YOST

Post Hill
PRESS

A POST HILL PRESS BOOK
ISBN: 978-1-63758-841-3
ISBN (eBook): 978-1-63758-842-0

Justify This:
A Career Without Compromise
© 2024 by Nick Fear Incorporated
All Rights Reserved

Cover design by Conroy Accord

Post Hill Press
New York • Nashville
posthillpress.com

Published in the United States of America
1 2 3 4 5 6 7 8 9 10

For James and Marie
For Mitzi
For Chloe and Omar
For Leslie, without whom I am nothing
and
For Rush

CONTENTS

FOREWORD (FROM THE LEFT) BY GRAHAM YOST SHOWRUNNER, *JUSTIFIED*

When Nick asked me to write a foreword for his book, I was surprised. Usually, he only reaches out to chastise me for not having cast him in anything recently. But no, turns out, he'd *actually written* a book. About himself. Actors, right? I asked if I could read it before I wrote a foreword because I was concerned that it might get a little, ahem...*political*. So he sent the book, and by page 1, it was clear—it's a *lot* political.

Why on earth would Nick ask *me* to write a foreword? I mean, I'm Canadian. Given where Nick falls on the spectrum, I'm sure he thinks Canada is a socialist dictatorship where citizens are forced to worship Wayne Gretzky and Joni Mitchell (though, c'mon, Wayne wasn't called "the Great One" for nothing, and Joni's "A Case of You" is the best grown-up breakup song ever written).

Did Nick ask me to write this simply because I cast him on *Justified* and gave him the best job of his career? Or, did he ask me because he wanted to troll a Canadian lib?

Either way, I said yes. Though what I've written isn't so much a foreword as a *rebuttal*.

Not about politics. Heavens no. Nick and I *never* talked politics. Maybe he told me he was backing Herman Cain at one point, but that was about it. What we talked about were our lives, our children, the business we're in. So, it's not his politics I want to rebut, but how I'm portrayed (or *not* portrayed) in this book.

Look, I'm as much of a Hollywood a-hole as the rest of them. When I find out someone I know has written an autobiography, I flip to the index to see if I'm in it. Nick's book didn't have an index when he sent it to me (and may not have one in the version you're reading now), so I had to read the whole blasted thing!

I'm kidding. I skimmed it. I slowed down at the part where he got his big break in *Fried Green Tomatoes* (directed by our friend Jon Avnet, whom I just mentioned to make sure he gets into the index). I *really* slowed down when it got to the parts about *From the Earth to the Moon* and *Justified*.

[SPOILER ALERT: I am going to mention things that Nick probably wanted you to first read about later in the book.]

Now, maybe I didn't slow enough, and maybe I missed it, but in his *Earth to the Moon* section, my name doesn't appear *once*. It's all Tom-this and Tom-that (mostly Hanks; a little Sizemore). Uh, Nick? I was a producer on that miniseries. I won an Emmy for it. I was nominated for writing the episode about Apollo 1. I directed the one about the building of the lunar lander. Apparently, according to Nick's omissions, those episodes just wrote, produced, and directed themselves. [And yes, I will gratuitously flaunt my credits. Not unlike a friend I have who will work into any conversation the fact that he once subbed for Rush Limbaugh.]

After the *Earth to the Moon* section, I skipped through a bunch of stuff in the book until Nick got to *Justified*. What Nick writes there is pretty accurate: I told him I cast him as Chief Deputy US Marshal Art Mullen because I was tired of his Christmas card every year having a note asking why I hadn't put him in anything lately. It's also true when he claims a famous line in the show was a line he improvised (it's in the pilot, where Art equates Raylan's reputation for shooting people with a kindergartener getting a reputation as a biter).

The problem is, Nick takes that one improvised line and makes it sound like *all* the best lines were his. In seventy-eight episodes over six seasons, Nick probably had a thousand lines, but he doesn't say, "Thanks for the great words, Graham! You and the other writers sure did a bang-up job of bringing Elmore Leonard's world to life!" Nah. What I get is: "You like that biter line? That was *me*!"

When I said I wanted to cast him as Art Mullen, FX and Sony pushed back. Not because they didn't like Nick, but because it was the very first part cast for the pilot and they wanted to be sure. So our great casting director, Cami Patton (also now in the index!), suggested Conor O'Farrell (index!) come in and read for the part. I knew Conor and loved his work. He'd also been in *Earth to the Moon*, playing Jim McDivitt, the commander of Apollo 9. I directed the episode which covered the Apollo 9 mission. The first scene up on the first day of filming was a scene between Nick and Conor. As I said to Cami, no matter who FX chooses, we'll get someone playing Art who was in the first scene I ever directed. As it happened, FX backed my preference for Nick (and Conor appeared later in the series, in a recurring role as an ATF agent).

But there's a little more to the story. I didn't pick Nick for the part when I wrote the *Justified* pilot, I picked him for the part *months* before, when I first read Elmore's novella, *Fire in the Hole*. I got to the first scene where Art Mullen appeared and I thought, "This should be Nick Searcy." And the truth is, no matter what FX or Sony said, Nick was going to be Art, even if it meant I had to stomp my feet and hold my breath until they caved. I mean, even if they'd said they wanted Matt Damon for the part and Matt agreed to do it, I would've... Okay, I would've gone with Matt Damon, I'm not an idiot.

I wanted Nick for the part for a bunch of reasons. First, he's a terrific actor. He's real, he's smart, and he's very, very funny—and any show based on the writing of Elmore Leonard had better be funny. I also knew that having him around would be good for the show. He takes the work seriously but carries it lightly—he knows only too well how lucky any of us are to make a living in this business. This book really shows what it's like to be a working actor. The ups and downs, the ins and outs. The joy, and the panic.

So, back to the original questions: Why did Nick ask me to write this foreword and why did I say yes? For my part, I said yes because Nick is a friend and he is a good man, and I have a feeling he feels the same about me. Again, unless he's just trolling a lib.

I honestly hope this book sells a million copies, so Nick never has to work again. Or will at least never have to whine about me not casting him every year in his Season's Greetings card. And yes, I just called it a Season's Greetings card. *That's* how you troll someone in their own book.

FOREWORD (FROM THE RIGHT) BY LARRY CORREIA
AUTHOR, *MONSTER HUNTER INTERNATIONAL* SERIES

Most of you got to know Nick Searcy through some of his many film and TV roles. I got to know Nick by beating the crap out of angsty socialists on Twitter with him. Over the years, we tag-team debated against congressmen, reporters, professors, and hundreds of other assorted America-hating goofballs. Alone, we still had them outnumbered, but with a couple of us fighting, we had them totally surrounded.

Like Nick, I'm an anomaly in my career field. I'm a novelist, and just like everybody in Hollywood is supposed to be a good-thinking proper liberal, the same thing is expected in publishing. For a long time, everybody who was Other-Than-Liberal kept their heads down and their mouths shut out of fear of committing career suicide. The accepted narrative was that everybody in the entertainment industries believed the same approved way. Anybody who diverged from the progressive playbook—like icky conservatives or libertarians—had better keep quiet if they knew what was good for them.

In reality, creatives are just as politically and philosophically divided as the rest of the country, but in the entertainment business, the nail that sticks up gets hammered down.

Whether you are working in movies, TV, video games, comic books, novels, tabletop games, cartoons, YouTubing, podcasting, whatever, it doesn't matter... First, the Left pretends we don't exist, and then they cancel, sabotage, blackball, and squash whichever ones won't shut up. They simply can't abide dissent.

It's like a bad mafia trope. "Hey, that's a nice career you've got there. It would be a real shame if something bad were to happen to it."

Some of us, however, are just pathologically incapable of being good little serfs. I don't know if it is some sort of oppositional defiance disorder, or we just really can't stand BS, but a handful of outspoken creatives won't be shamed into silence. You can't browbeat us into surrendering. We're going to stand up for what we believe, regardless of the cost.

With Nick, I found a fellow traveler. Here was a successful working actor who agreed with the not-crazy half of America, and he was open about it! *In public!*

Every single day, I'd watch as somebody new would come along to try to browbeat, shame, or insult Nick into falling in line. But nope, Nick wouldn't bend. The handful who engaged in good faith, he'd treat them with respect. The vast mob who came in howling for blood, Nick would meet them head-on, guns blazing, no quarter given.

This is a man who has brought intensity and passion to an incredible variety of roles. He can play the righteous good guy or a terrifying villain. Drama, comedy, it doesn't matter, because Nick always makes his characters feel like real people. When Nick plays a role, that character feels like somebody you could meet in real life standing in line at the grocery store, or working on the space program, or hunting down a fugitive. He's even talented enough to play a very convincing Democrat.

Nick Searcy is a fantastic actor, but more importantly, he's a great American. He's a husband and father who wants what's best for his family and country. That honest conviction bleeds through. He's a North Carolina boy who never forgot where he came from.

While the public actions of certain snooty Hollywood elitists have made it so that most Americans think of actors as vapid, sheltered, bossy, know-it-alls, many of the working stiffs in Hollywood are just regular people who are as sick of the corruption and stupidity in Washington, DC as the rest of us.

The difference between most of them and Nick is that he's willing to put it on the line.

The only thing necessary for the triumph of evil is for good men to do nothing. That quote is usually attributed to the philosopher and statesman Edmund Burke, but regardless of who first said it, it remains true. We got into the situation we are now, where one side dominates the culture and bullies compliance, because too many good people were afraid to stand up and say, "This is really dumb."

But Nick's not just some activist who puts the message ahead of his art. He gets that the story comes first. An author friend of mine, whom I will not name because he's politically moderate and would probably get screamed at by caring liberals just for being mentioned here, once said something to the effect that you should never preach harder than you entertain.

At the end of the day, we are entertainers. It's our job to bring some joy into the audience's world. Too many creatives decide to be activists first, entertainers second. They think it's their job to yell at the audience and make them feel stupid and uncomfortable. That's one big reason so many recent Hollywood productions flop. Half the country is sick of being yelled at.

There's a lot of power in story, and for too long the Right side of the political divide was happy to abdicate the entertainment business to the Left. Movies? Books? Games? That wasn't serious business! Important ideas can only be conveyed through talk shows and think tanks! Then they were baffled why the Left totally owned the culture, and across all media Republicans were usually portrayed as backwards, racist, dorks until gullible people bought fully into that narrative. We're still reaping the effects of that bad call to this day.

Story matters. Entertainment matters. Like Andrew Breitbart said, politics really is downstream of culture.

Nick Searcy gets that better than anybody.

EXCERPTS FROM "POLITICS IN HOLLYWOOD," SPEECH DELIVERED BY NICK SEARCY, HILLSDALE COLLEGE LEADERSHIP CONFERENCE NAPLES, FLORIDA, FEBRUARY 20, 2020

Hello, my friends, and thank you so much for having me. Actors aren't usually allowed in polite society, and for good reason, so I do appreciate the sacrifice…

As excited as I am to be here today, I can't imagine how excited you must be. I know everyone here is very worried about what Hollywood thinks about you. Let me just say at the outset, most of the time we don't think about you at all. We're too busy thinking about ourselves, right? Thinking about things like, "Do these yoga pants make me look fat?" And, "Hmm, maybe I should get this mole taken off my face." That sort of thing.

That's what they're generally thinking about. It's not you. But I know it probably keeps you up at night wondering, "Why don't the people who were friends of Harvey Weinstein's think I'm a good person?" That's why I'm here today. With apologies to Ronald Reagan, the eight most terrifying words in the English language are: "I'm from Hollywood, and I'm here to help."

Being an outlier, I'm usually asked a lot of questions, and one of the things I'm usually asked is, "Why is Hollywood the way it is? Why is it so monolithically Left, especially when they are in one of the most directly transactional capitalist businesses in the world?" I mean, show business is really just an episode of *The Little Rascals* where Spanky and Alfalfa want to put on a show for the neighborhood. They're going to charge five cents, and if it's a good show, they'll make money, and if it's a bad show, they will fail. That's what Hollywood basically is.

It's pure capitalism. Why don't they understand that? Well, there are various answers to this question, but I want to tell you one story about my first cousin Gary. When I first moved to Hollywood in the 1980s, my cousin Gary came out to visit me, and Gary was in the weaving business. He made rugs and went all over the world with this business. He did very well with it, and when he was out in Los Angeles for a trade show, he met me one night for a few drinks, and he said, "You know what, Nick? I've got Los Angeles and Hollywood figured out. I know why everything is so screwed up here."

And I said, "Well, tell me what it is."

And he says, "Well, for a hundred years, the craziest people in America have moved to Hollywood to try to become movie stars, and some of them made it, and those crazy people had kids, and so on."

For a second, I was wondering if he was including me in that.

But I also think there's a certain amount of groupthink and intimidation going on here. Because it's so difficult to get a job in this business that the sheer numbers are just completely unfavorable to a newcomer. It's practically impossible. The late great comedian Louis C. K. had a great line about this. I mean, he's not really dead, he's just canceled. Leftist-on-leftist action is just irresistible to me; I can't stop watching it. But he had a great line about it, and it was: "Saying that you want to be a professional actor is like saying that you want to be a cartoon dog wearing a jet pack. It is just about as likely." There are so many reasons that a given actor doesn't get a job: You're too fat. You're too thin. You're too old. You're too smart. (The too smart and too handsome reason is given to me a lot.)

You want to give them as few reasons as possible to reject you, right? So it makes more sense to join the Club, and that's what the bullies who are the enforcers in Hollywood do here. They speak out publicly and constantly to send out the signal that if you want to be in this business, you have to join the (left-wing) Club.

In a perfect example, take a Presidential Medal of Freedom recipient, Robert De Niro. You thought I was going to say Rush Limbaugh, didn't you? Did I mention that I guest-hosted for Rush once? I don't know if I mentioned that. But anyway, Barack Obama gave De Niro the same Medal of Freedom, the same medal that President Trump gave Mr. Limbaugh. But of course, when Trump gave it to Rush, he made all the Democrats watch it happen during the State of the Union, which is one more reason to love President Trump. But at the Tony Awards in 2018, Robert De Niro got up onstage and thought it'd be perfectly fine to repeatedly yell, "Duck Trump."

I said "Duck" with a "D." He didn't say that; he said something else. He's called Donald Trump a gangster, he's called him Hitler, has called him racist and white supremacist. You know, all the same things that Democrats call every single Republican president and every presidential candidate going back to even Romney and McCain when they tried to convince us that they wanted to beat Obama.

But Mr. De Niro also made headlines when he said he hoped President Trump would be hit in the face with a flying bag of excrement, although he didn't say "excrement" either. And just bear in mind when he says things like that, he really wants to hit everybody who voted for Trump in the face. That's a lot of excrement, so it's a good thing the Democrats have San Francisco—they're going need it.

People are always asking me: Why do these actors do this? Why do they repeatedly just go out of their way to insult the entire Trump electorate? Well, the first thing is, I truly believe, that it's to intimidate. They want to intimidate everybody into believing that if you want to be in show business, you've got to support the Democrats. You've got to hate the Republicans. There's been a lot of talk in the last few years within the circles of conservative Hollywood—which is a very small and intimate circle—about whether or not there is actually a blacklist. And the fear of this blacklist is what led to the establishment of the top-secret conservative fellowship group in Los Angeles that you probably have all heard of, so it's not so secret, called Friends of Abe. But for most of the Obama years, this group was a safe haven for actors and writers and people like me who aren't leftists and don't believe arguments like, "Real socialism has never been tried." This group functioned like an AA meeting for Republicans. It was like, we would all get together, and we'd stand up and go, "Hi, my name is Nick, and (voice cracks) I'm a Republican."

I miss that group. But while there may not be an actual blacklist, it doesn't really matter. There doesn't need to be, because Hollywood is a town that's run by fear and filled with cowards, and a whisper campaign is all it takes. All the decisions are also made by committee. So, fourteen people have to sign off on every actor they cast, especially if it's in a major role. If just one person in that room goes, "I don't like that guy," that's it. They don't even have to say why. They don't have to say, "I don't want Nick Searcy to do it because he voted for Trump, and he's not ashamed of it."

All they have to say is, "I think we can do better than him." And when Trump was elected, he tore the masks off of everybody, which was one of his superpowers. The leftists in Hollywood don't even bother to hide it anymore. They blast their fascist tendencies all over the media, and they do that knowing that they're going to get more work, not less. They're going to get more work if they do that.

For example, when a Trump fundraiser in Beverly Hills was announced a few years ago, Will and Grace got involved. You remember *Will & Grace*? I wish I didn't. But Debra Messing felt comfortable asking for names. She tweeted, "Please print a list of all attendees, the public has a right to know. And then we'll get involved." And Eric McCormack tweeted, "Hey, @THR [the *Hollywood Reporter*], kindly report on everyone attending this event, so the rest of us can be clear about who we don't wanna work with. Thx." At least he said thanks.

Will and Grace are just the tip of the iceberg. However, there are so many well-known actors you would recognize by face, if not by name, who say to me all the time, "Man, I agree with you. But I would never say it out loud, because I know it will hurt my bottom line, and you're crazy." And they are undoubtedly correct and smarter than me. But Hollywood used to make a movie about McCarthyism about every fifteen minutes. It's like their favorite subject. De Niro himself made one called *Guilty by Suspicion* in 1991.

The reason it's one of their favorite subjects is that it allows leftists to paint themselves as the abused victims of the evil Republicans, even though it was their own colleagues in Hollywood who blacklisted them. It wasn't Congress. It was the people they worked with. So why do they act in real life like the bad guys in their movies that they make? It's because they're rewarded for it. If you make some vile, ignorant, hateful statement about a Republican, it will be considered a resume enhancement in Hollywood that shows you're in the Club and shows you're one of them.

It's better than an audition. It's better than a billboard on Sunset Boulevard, and the more hateful it is, the better. The more Alec Baldwin attacks Trump, the more Emmy nominations he gets. That's the way it works. And they never pay a price for it. They are insulated from paying a price for it. If you're a name that producers are willing to pay millions of dollars for, like De Niro, you're considered royalty, and no one in Hollywood can say excrement to you.

The studios have protected themselves, too, by cross-collateralizing everything. For example: if you feel like watching *Game of Thrones*, and you subscribe to HBO, you're also subsidizing Bill Maher and *Vice* and countless documentaries about how wonderful Nancy Pelosi is and how awful Republicans are. And that's just the way they've done it. They can make one *Avengers* movie that makes a billion dollars, and that gives them a chance to make a bunch of other movies that they're just making for each other. They're just making them to show off and say, "Look, I'm in the Club. Look how woke I am; look at this movie." That's how it works.

So the message gets sent. If you want to succeed, you have to be in the Club, and if you aren't in the Club, they're not going to let you in. If you have a story that you want to tell, or a movie that you want to make, and it doesn't fit their ideology, they won't touch it. Either they won't touch it, or they'll put you in a box. A lot of the studios have created these boxes that are for faith-based films, and so they put it over there and say we're going to make these films for "those" people, because they'll probably pay for it. But we don't want them to be associated with our mainstream films.

They put it over to the side so they can make a little money on it. But they've identified it, and they've targeted it, and they've dismissed it. The ultimate effect is that they are marching down the field of culture unopposed. The Left never wants to win fair and square. They can't do it. They can't win on their ideas, so they have to clear the field. That's why they want to silence everybody who speaks out against them, and they don't want to have movies made that are against their ideology.

They throw the word *fascism* around, while they probably couldn't define it if their next government check depended on it, because they are the fascists, and they don't realize it.

So what this all means is we as conservatives have got to get in this game somehow. We have got to get in the field of entertainment. We've got to put the pads on and the helmet on and get out there and hit somebody. Like my football coach in high school used to say, "You know, those people over there on the other side of the field, they put their pants on one leg at a time just like we do. They don't run and jump into them. They're just like us." So that's how we've got to look at the Hollywood Left. We're just as good at it as they are, but the Left has had this long march through the institutions virtually unopposed.

Three years ago, the Democrat Party was on the verge of nominating a full-blown unashamed communist for president. They were close to nominating Bernie Sanders. And when you see all these young lunatics who are at the Sanders rallies, ripping their shirts off and grabbing the microphone from him, you have to wonder: How did this happen? How did we get to this point where we have so many historically ignorant young people who embrace socialism?

Well, my friend Jesse Kelly, who's a top radio show host out of Houston, explains it like this: "Start going to a government school at the age of six. Keep going until you're twenty and spend seven hours a day learning how bad America sucks, and almost nothing about the deadly evils of communism, and then you'll understand Bernie Sanders." So now, if you add on the fact that every bit of mainstream entertainment that they consume from the time they're old enough to watch *Teletubbies*, it reinforces the same ideas. Republicans are racist, Christians are hypocrites, progressivism is compassionate. America is evil and imperialist. That's the message that is constantly beat into their heads."

But there is a vastly underserved audience out there that has an appetite for entertainment that does not demean them or demean our country. We have to find a delivery system for it. A couple of years ago, I directed a movie that did go around the system called *Gosnell*, which is a movie about the real-life case of abortion doctor Kermit Gosnell, who was convicted in Philadelphia in 2013 for multiple crimes, including murder, for snipping the necks of babies after they had been born—which is now legal in New York.

We had to go around the system. The money was successfully raised on Indiegogo in 2014. We shot it in 2015. The movie was finished by early to mid-2016, and it took nearly two and a half years to find a distributor to release the movie in October of 2018. And we had a very reputable sales agent on board. He had sold a lot of movies in the past, and he watched the finished film. He said, "This is a good movie, and it should sell very quickly."

He got one offer for only fifty thousand dollars, and he got responses like this: "It's a good movie. And I'm sure there's an audience for it. But I have to work with these people on Monday." So, the distribution companies were afraid that they'd be kicked out of the Club if they were involved with *Gosnell*. And then our advertising dates got pushed back. Facebook blocked our ads. NPR refused to run ads that contained the words *abortion doctor*. Lifetime and Hallmark, two networks whose audience would intersect with our audience, wouldn't run any of the ads. The only network that would take our ads was Fox News. And we got some airtime from talk radio hosts like Glenn Beck, who gave us a great hour-long spot, and my close personal friend Rush talked about the movie. Did I mention that I guest-hosted for Rush? Even given all that resistance, *Gosnell*, when it was released in six hundred theaters, was the number-one indie film in the country that weekend, and we cracked the top ten overall.

The reviews were typically polarized: half of them hated it, half of them loved it. The ones who hated it slammed it as right-wing propaganda, of course, but the really surprising thing was the number of reviews. Films released generally in six hundred or more theaters always get at least one hundred reviews, and some get up to two hundred. *Gosnell* got eleven reviews. Eleven. And they ultimately treated the movie like they treated the actual Gosnell case and trial, which is they just ignored it. They pretended that it didn't exist.

We tried to make a film that was based as much as possible on actual court transcripts and direct interviews with the principal real-life players and tried to stay close to the facts, because we didn't want to be dismissed as propaganda. But guess what? They called it propaganda anyway.

The Left isn't interested in having facts be out there. The entire subject of abortion is something they don't want to talk about. The only thing you need to know about abortion in the Hollywood narrative is that if you oppose it or even want restrictions on it, you are a racist who hates women, and you can't be in the Club. That's it. So, if we want to tell our story, we've got to build a new Hollywood, because this one is broken.

And I don't just mean content. We have to build a delivery system to bring the content to the audience that wants to see it. I think the first step we have to take to achieve this is that we as conservatives have got to recognize the power of storytelling. The Left has dominated that field forever. Conservative investors are generally not disposed towards financing feature films or television shows that aren't documentaries.

It's not just because they're risky investments, which they are, but it's because we don't perceive the value of storytelling. Jesus Christ spoke in parables. He didn't come out and just say, "Here are the facts people"—although he did do that sometimes, but he mostly taught through storytelling. And that's what we have to do, and that's what we have to learn. Conservatives like to fund news networks, but they don't like to fund sitcoms, because they don't see the value in it. A friend of mine put it like this: If the conservatives were building a library, it would be all nonfiction. And if the liberals were building a library, it would all be novels and poems and short stories. And of course, the liberal library would be a lot more fun to visit. That's where I would go, because it'd be a lot more popular because storytelling is popular. Storytelling helps people learn. I'm about to use one of the most overused quotes in twenty-first-century conservative speeches, but that's not going to stop me.

Andrew Breitbart once famously said, "Politics is downstream of culture." We have let the Hollywood Left define the culture for at least fifty years. But we have an opening now because Hollywood has destroyed itself. They've revealed themselves by expressing their seething contempt for everyone who disagrees with them. They've alienated themselves from a large portion of America, because now when someone from Middle America hears the words *movie star*, they don't automatically think, *Oh, that's someone beautiful and handsome who acts in movies and makes me feel emotions.* No, we don't think that anymore. When somebody hears *movie star*, it's like, "Oh, yeah, it's just another idiot who hates me because I won't vote for socialism."

They've really left us a huge opening. So how do we do it? How do we build a new Hollywood? Well, my idea is that the entertainment business needs its own Rush Limbaugh (whose show I guest-hosted on December 27, 2017). But here's what I mean by that. It's really hard for people who weren't alive back then to understand what life was like before Rush Limbaugh, because there was no one—and I mean no one—like him. There was no Fox News. There was no Hannity. There wasn't even really talk radio as a national format. There was no alternative to the alphabet networks and the biased news reporting that they do, and Rush, by himself, pretty much destroyed the monopoly that the Left had on the news business, and his effect on the culture has been immeasurable.

And that's why the Left tried and failed for thirty years to destroy him, because they knew how effective he was. Rush changed Andrew Breitbart; Rush changed *me*. And basically, we have to accept the fact that we are the counterculture now, not them, not Hollywood. We are the Sex Pistols, people. We are the punk rockers, and we need to pick up this mantle. I always think if Rush Limbaugh had existed during the Nixon years, that President Nixon might not have resigned. He might have just thought, *Hey, that guy's on the radio fighting. Maybe I'll fight too.*

I would also argue right now that without Rush, there would have been no President Trump. That's how much he changed the culture. And speaking of President Trump, one of the reasons that the Left is so ineffective against him, and why they hate him so much, is that President Trump comes from the culture. He doesn't come from politics. He comes from the celebrity culture. He had a reality show for years, and the American people got comfortable with him. They got to know him a little bit. And they got a sense that this is a real person. He's not a focus-group phony like almost every single politician that we've encountered before, like (enter any politician's name here).

Similar to Rush, Trump does not filter himself. He doesn't put on airs. He doesn't focus-group his thoughts. He just talks to us and tells us what he thinks, whether it's on social media platforms or whether it was when he used to walk to the helicopter on the White House lawn going, "No, you're fake news. Fake News. No, shut up. No, not you. Don't be rude. Don't be rude."

But in closing, what we really need is a Rush Limbaugh of entertainment. And I have an idea about who that should be…

By the way, did I mention that I am the biggest Hollywood star to have ever guest-hosted the Rush Limbaugh program?

I'm from Hollywood, and I'm here to help. Good night, everybody!

⬚ CHAPTER 1 ⬚

MY BIG BREAKS BEGIN

The first in my long series of big breaks began in 1959, when I was born to two wonderful people, James and Marie Searcy, in the most beautiful place on Earth, western North Carolina. I was born in Hendersonville, but grew up in a town called Cullowhee. It was a college town, home to the Catamounts of Western Carolina University. My mother was a biology teacher (and perhaps the most popular and beloved teacher in Cullowhee High School history), and my father was a contractor, an accountant, a basketball coach, and, for six years, the Jackson County accountant. The scenic backdrop of the Smoky Mountains presented a beautiful environment to grow up in, and living in a college town like Cullowhee gave me some opportunities that I may not have had if I lived a bit further away from civilization.

I remember when I was in the fifth grade, folks from the theater department of the university came down to my school and said they were looking for a child who might be interested in acting, and all the teachers pointed at me and said, "Get that Searcy kid. He's been doing Tom Jones impressions for show-and-tell in front of the class." And they ended up casting me. They were doing a play called *Coming Through the Rye*, written by William Saroyan. It was a little one-act play about people in purgatory, waiting to go to heaven or hell, and I played a twelve-year-old boy who was trying to figure out why he died. That was my first experience with being an actor, and I just fell in love with it. I knew that that's what I wanted to do with my life when I was twelve years old.

I remember the very moment that I decided. I was watching *The Mary Tyler Moore Show*, which I loved, in the basement of my house, and I thought to myself, "Those people look like they are having so much fun. I want to do that."

Unfortunately, there was no drama department at my high school, and during my sophomore, junior, and senior years, I just made people do plays with me. I got my English teacher, Melba Simpson, to sponsor the play, and I would put on the show. I remember doing *The Zoo Story* by Edward Albee in the school cafeteria—not exactly dinner theatre material, if you know what I mean. I began reading plays, watching TV more seriously, and—always—going to the movies. The closest theater to me was the Ritz Theatre in Sylva, North Carolina, and they would run two films a week—one film on Sunday, Monday, and Tuesday, then a different film on Wednesday, Thursday, Friday, Saturday. I don't think I missed one. My parents would just drop me off at the theatre and pick me up after.

I went to all of them, no matter what the film was about. I remember seeing a film called *Jackson County Jail*, with Tommy Lee Jones and Yvette Mimieux. It was Tommy Lee Jones's first or second film. When I saw Tommy Lee Jones, I thought, *Well, that guy's not very good looking, but he's a professional actor. Maybe I could do that.* The whole notion that you have to be some good-looking matinee idol, soap opera type went out the window for me after seeing that. I thought, *Hmm, okay, you can be a normal-looking person and still be an actor.* Gene Hackman was also an inspiration to me in that way—and strangely enough, I wound up working with both of them!

At the time, being an actor on TV or in the movies seemed as far-fetched and distant as the Earth was to the Moon. There was no pathway. I didn't know how to do it and make it a reality. No one did. When I told my parents I wanted to be an actor, they weren't unsupportive, but they were rightfully skeptical. Growing up in Cullowhee, North Carolina in the '60s and '70s, we didn't know one person who had become a professional actor. Was it even possible?

But I was persistent and determined. I think that trait runs in my extended family. I also was exposed to performances at a young age. A number of my uncles, and at least three of my first cousins, are preachers. I went to a lot of revivals and sermons in my youth, and I think watching them onstage got into my blood a little bit, and by that I mean the Message as well as the way it was delivered. For a while, I thought I wanted to be a preacher, but then I realized that what I really liked was how people shut up and listened to them. They were telling a powerful story and making people want to hear it. And that was what I wanted to do. I wanted to be a storyteller.

Acting also interested me because it felt like a way to experience more than one life. When I was young, I read so many books and I had so many different interests, that I felt like I didn't want to be just *one thing*—like just a lawyer, or a doctor, or an athlete. I wanted to have *more than one life*, as crazy as that sounds. Playing different characters, imagining myself living the life of another person, even if it was just for a week or a month or two and even if I was just pretending, made me feel like my life would be richer. The whole idea sounds rather crazy and juvenile to me now, but it really did drive me—and it many ways, I think it served me. And in many ways it still serves me.

Perhaps the most important thing that shaped me was being blessed with a mother, Marie Searcy, who constantly told me my entire life that I could be *anything* I wanted to be. She made me fearless, and willing to try anything. She's why I learned to play the piano, why I became a good basketball player, why I played trombone, ran for class president, why I became valedictorian, on and on. Once she said to me, early in my career, when I was struggling to get started, "I don't know why you chose the most difficult profession on earth!"

And I said, "Mom, it's all your fault. You told me I could do anything, and I believed you!"

All in all, I had a spectacular childhood in Cullowhee, North Carolina. I went K-12 all in the same building, Camp Laboratory School/Cullowhee High School, where my mother taught biology. Being in such a small school, so close to a University, afforded me so many varied opportunities. I was in a rock band, played trombone in the school concert band, on the clogging team, on the basketball team, on the football team, and even edited the school yearbook my senior year, on and on. I developed a love for English literature, for classical music, as well as being a two sport athlete. My valedictory address talked about how unique the environment we had grown up in was, with most of our class having been together for 12 years. That address resonated with many people and is still close to my heart.

When I got out of high school, my parents weren't necessarily insistent that I go to college: It was just assumed that that's what I was going to do. They really wanted me to go to the University of North Carolina, because that was, for them, the pinnacle of achievement. I was considered for the Morehead Scholarship at UNC, and a number of other scholarships (I *was* class valedictorian *and* a star basketball player—in a graduating class of 55, as my wife always reminds me). But, as fate would have it, I didn't get any of the scholarships. At the last minute, I said what I wanted to do was audition for the North Carolina School of the Arts, in Winston-Salem, which offered four-year degrees in only five subjects: drama, dance, music, visual arts, and design and production. At that point I don't think the school had been around for more than three or four years. I was accepted there, and entered the actor's training program.

To say I had a bit of culture shock when I arrived on campus would be an understatement. I might as well have arrived on another planet. Everyone around me was talking another language. I didn't know what was going on. The department head was Malcolm Morrison, who came from the Royal Academy of Dramatic Arts (RADA), and NCSA had the Royal Academy philosophy whereby you as a young actor don't know anything, can't do anything, and you have to be torn down to nothing and completely rebuilt in their image.

As freshmen, we were told we had to wear leotards and tights to all our classes, even to academic electives, like philosophy or music theory. We were all sitting there in our leotards and tights, and we had to wear them all day long. I mean, you can imagine how bad these things smelled after a while. The whole thing just seemed insane.

They kept harping on my Southern accent, and I honestly thought, "I don't know what you're talking about. I sound like Paul Newman. I've been practicing in the mirror. Y'all are the ones that sound weird."

Needless to say, I really didn't fit in. Acting began to seem like something I just didn't want to do. I thought, *If this is what being an actor is, I don't want to be one.* I thought I was going to go to this school to study drama and put on plays like I had been doing, which was a lot of fun. There wasn't any of that as a freshman.

We went to voice class, and speech class, and music theory class, and movement class, and learned the Alexander Technique—all rather strange and ultimately incomprehensible to an 18-year-old mountain boy. In the middle of the second semester, Dean Morrison called me in to his office and informed me, "We don't feel like you're progressing very well, and we're not sure you're going to be invited back next year." At that point, I decided to quit before I was fired.

I immediately applied to the University of North Carolina, just beating the admission deadline, and was accepted. I thought, "Let's start over. I'm going to be a freshman at the University of North Carolina. Basically, I wasted a year of my life to go to an arts school and I now realize those people are crazy."

(Years later, a real scandal erupted at NCSA that began when I was there. Some of the faculty were having sexual escapades with some of the students, and there were lawsuits, firings, and various repercussions. I had no idea that was happening when I was there. When I heard about it, I thought, *What the hell? Why didn't any of them come after me? What am I, chopped liver?*)

But many good things came from my experiences at NCSA. My roommate during my time at NCSA was a fellow classmate in the drama department named Frank Garrett, who at that time was simply the strangest person I had ever met. He was an antique dealer who had a wind-up Victrola phonograph in our dorm room, on which he constantly played 78s from the 1920s and '30s. I didn't know what to think of this crazy person when I first met him, but by the time I left, we were the best of friends, and we remain so to this day.

Frank was the first person I ever met who made his own films. He shot his films on Super 8 and edited them himself with a manual film splicer, literally gluing the film together before running it through the projector. We made a film together there before I left, entitled *Mr. Garrett and Nick Go to a Party*, heavily influenced by Laurel and Hardy, whom Frank revered. This led me after I left to make many of my own Super 8 classics, the most ambitious of which, *The Incredible Screaming Man*, was an epic thirteen-minute sound film about a flesh-craving maniac who starved to death because everyone could hear him coming a mile away since he couldn't stop screaming.

I will always be indebted to my friend Frank. If I had never met him, I don't know if I ever would have directed a film. He taught me to love the medium—as well as making me a lifelong Laurel and Hardy fan, which I have passed along to my brilliant daughter, Chloe. The year at NCSA was invaluable to me because of the friendship and influence of Frank.

In 1978, I started all over again in Chapel Hill, and it was like being released from prison. I felt like I could do anything. I even decided to try out for the JV basketball team. I had lost quite a bit of weight at School of the Arts and was in much better shape than I was when I was MVP at Cullowhee High School. I did well at the first tryout, but I began to feel like I didn't want to go back to being a full-time athlete. The coach had cut the tryout squad from sixty guys to thirty, and I saw that I had made the posted list. I was supposed to initial it, to say I was coming back for the second round, but I decided not to continue.

The JV coach actually called me and asked me to come in to his office. He asked me why I didn't want to come back. I told him that my heart just wasn't in it, I felt like there wasn't really a future for me in basketball, and I didn't want to take someone else's spot who really loved it. I had so many other interests, and when you play basketball at a university, it is ALL you do. You don't have time for anything else. The coach tried to talk me into staying, told me he thought I had a real chance to make the team, and asked me to think about it.

I did, and I never went back. (Years later, I was watching ESPN in my crummy New York City apartment, and a story came on about the new head coach at Kansas, who was the former JV coach at North Carolina. And I went, "Hey, it's that guy who tried to talk me into playing basketball!" It was Roy Williams. To this day, I wish I had just gone ahead and played. At least for one year.)

But not playing gave me the time to throw myself into campus life. Thomas Wolfe, author of *Look Homeward Angel*, was a hero of mine, and I was thrilled to be walking the same paths in Chapel Hill that he had walked. I focused on my writing and wrote a lot of poetry, which was another passion of mine. Not playing basketball gave me time to try a lot of things on campus. I was even in the marching band my freshman year, playing baritone horn for the Marching Tar Heels at the football games. I met a really great piano player named Scott Green, and we started putting on hour long concerts in the Quad during lunch once in a while, playing Dan Fogelberg and Jackson Browne and Billy Joel songs for people going to class. This was the first time I became lead singer instead of always accompanying myself on the piano. We worked up to the point where we added a drummer and a bass player, and called ourselves *Nick Searcy and the 3-Day Band*.

Toward the end of my freshman year, some of the people I had met around campus and in classes were playwrights. One of them was a sophomore, Deanna Riley, and she asked me to be in a play she had written. So I did this little one-act play, and I ended up falling in love with the actress I was in it with, and I pretty much said to myself, "Okay, I want to be an actor again." We were together almost all through college up until my senior year, when we broke up.

But the culture of the drama department at UNC was exactly what I had wished NCSA had been. We took real acting classes—where you actually got to act, and not roll around on the floor in your leotard—and audition for plays. You could do three plays a semester if you wanted. I wound up doing at least two or three plays every semester, and I loved it. I played leading roles in mainstage productions of *Summer and Smoke, Hippolytus, The Would-Be Gentleman,* and many others. I played Romeo in *Romeo and Juliet,* and sang the role of Jesus in *Jesus Christ Superstar.* It was a tremendously fulfilling time in my life.

I had a journal in which I wrote down all the plays that I'd done. By the time I was a senior, I had almost fifty plays under my belt.

After graduation, it was time to reevaluate life again. *What happens now? What do I do?* Well, it just so happened that the girl I was dating at the time was from New York, and she had the grand notion of, "Let's go to New York and be actors."

But by that time, I had a full-fledged rock band, called Nick Fear. We billed ourselves as "The Most Terrifying Name in Rock and Roll," or sometimes "A Band Gone Mad with its Own Power." We played two hours of covers, specializing in Jackson Browne, Springsteen, Tom Petty, Elton John, Billy Joel, etc. Our biggest finale songs were *Born to Run* and *Running on Empty,* still my favorite song to play on the piano today.

We were a very theatrical band. I was the lead singer, and jumped around and acted a fool—very much like my Tom Jones impressions in the fifth grade. Our small but faithful following followed us around. We had various ways of staging our shows. One of my favorite tricks was to have the band go onstage without me, pretend like they didn't know where I was, and start playing our opening song, *Mercury Blues* by David Lindley, without me. I would talk one of the campus police into bringing me to the stage in handcuffs and uncuff me. I would jump onstage and perform, offering no explanation, sing for an hour, and at the end of the set, the policeman would come back and put the cuffs on me and take me away. Nick Fear was dangerous!

Nick Fear wasn't a big band, just me, a piano player, a drummer, a bass player, and a great guitar player named Andy York, who has gone on to be John Mellencamp's guitarist for the last thirty years. He made us pretty damn good. By the end of my senior year, we had added a saxophone player as well. For the first time, we were actually making a little money, playing in bars and not just for dormitory parties. So I decided to let my girlfriend go to New York without me, to see if we could make this band really take off. After graduation, I stayed in Chapel Hill for about three months.

But we were mostly playing bars and other small venues, for a couple hundred bucks a night. Split five ways, it wasn't much. And none of us could really write a song. I tried. I wrote a couple that were just…not good. I wrote a song called *We Don't Suck*, about my high school band. (But we did kind of suck, and so did the song.) We played these songs a couple of times, and then dropped them. I don't remember much about them except for one lyric, which went:

> *With a chronic case of oral diarrhea,*
> *We are cast adrift in a sea of ideas.*

As you can see, songwriting just wasn't my thing. It just didn't feel like a good path to continue down. And I began to realize that I wasn't really a great singer. I was just ACTING like a rock star, and Nick Fear was really just a character I was playing. It also dawned on me that being in a band was like having all your eggs in one basket, and you had to sell the whole basket, as one thing, whereas an acting career was a bit more flexible. If you didn't get one part, you go audition for another. There were more opportunities.

After a few months, my girlfriend asked again, "Well are you ready to move to New York with me now?" This time I jumped at the chance.

CHAPTER 2

BIG APPLE, BIG CHANCE

My parents, rightfully, had their concerns when I told them I was moving to New York, but they liked my girlfriend and were familiar with her. She had been over to the house a bunch of times, and my parents knew we were in a serious relationship that could potentially lead to marriage, so when I told them the news, they thought it was a bit crazy. They certainly weren't unsupportive, but they were skeptical—and had good reason to be.

New York in 1982 was absolute squalor (not that it's much different today—in many ways it's even worse now). It was a disaster, and we lived in a fairly nice area at that time. My girlfriend came from a wealthy family, but she was trying to prove herself to them and take care of herself financially, so she wasn't accepting any money from them. But at the same time, her family made sure she wasn't living in a really bad area, even though the neighborhood we were living in was referred to as Hell's Kitchen.

When I first arrived in New York, it was similar to when I first arrived at the arts school in the sense that nobody—and

I mean nobody—gave a *damn* about what I had done before I got there. And the culture shock took some time to get used to as well—learning which subways to ride, what times it was safe to go out, which neighborhoods not to go into, and the like. Times Square was an absolute hellhole at that time. It was far worse than any movie you've seen it portrayed in, and I *hated* it. I used to think Central Park was hell for bad trees. There were many, many times when I said to myself, "I'm going home! I can't stand it here!"

On top of that, I found myself in the hustle of trying to get an agent, trying to get somebody to pay attention to me, and trying to figure out how to break into the business. This was obviously long before the days of YouTube, where you can make a video and have it go viral. I suppose I could have made a VHS tape back then, but it would have been so primitive and had such a limited audience that it wouldn't have been worth the time or cost. Back then, the goal of an actor who moved to New York was to get in a play, have an agent or manager see you in that play, and hope they'd decide to represent you. That was the accepted pathway of becoming an actor at that time.

For my first two years in New York, I just didn't get anywhere and found myself doing odd jobs to earn an income. I was a limousine driver for a while and was just scraping by and not getting anywhere in my acting career. I'd get an off-off-off-Broadway play here and there, but it was always stuff I was doing for free. They were referred to as "showcase" gigs back then, and the odds of anyone of importance in the business "discovering" you were slim to none. But the experience was more valuable than anything else. It gave you a chance to practice your craft in front of an audience, which, more than anything else, is what actors need.

Backstage magazine was like a holy newsletter for beginning actors in those days. It would come out every week, and you'd skim through it looking for open auditions for everything from student films to big plays.

In 1983, I was cast in an off-off-Broadway play called *Dogs*, which was a musical take on the hit Broadway show *Cats*, and all the actors were dressed as dogs. (Yes, it was as ridiculous as it sounds.) I played a German shepherd named Boomie with a Texas drawl. The playwrights made my character sound that way so they wouldn't have to worry about my accent. My costume had Velcro testicles on it, which during the final song I would rip off and hold up for the audience, so they would know that I had been "fixed." The people producing the play were somehow very well financed and were able to bring the off-off-Broadway play to off-Broadway, which made me eligible to get into Actors' Equity. I was over the moon. I thought this was great. I was finally in the union!

After opening night was over, we all gathered at an apartment to watch a review of the play by Stewart Klein, who was a critic on New York's Channel 5, and had come to the play and was going to review it on-air. I thought, "This is great. He's going to give us a great review, and we're all going to be stars!"

They eventually cut to Stewart Klein, and his opening line was, "I went to see an off-Broadway play last night, called *Dogs*, and the only thing they forgot to do was spread newspaper on the stage before the play started."

Oh, shit! I knew we were doomed. I think we had nine performances after that before we closed. That was a crushing one.

After that, I wound up doing a few student films and little plays around 1984, and that was when I started feeling that I might be getting a little bit of a foothold. That's also around the time that I met my wife, the beautiful Leslie Riley, of Owensboro, Kentucky. We were cast in a play called *The Kennedy Play.*

It was a Pirandellian (it's a word, look it up) play about actors trying to create a play about the Kennedy family, in which the actors had a lot of license to improvise relationships with one another. So, my character improvised that I was in love with Leslie's character. As proof that I'm a good actor, she believed me, and I'm happy to report that we've been together ever since.

Leslie and I were both pretty poor at the time, the whole struggling-actor cliche. After weeks of pestering Leslie to go out with me after rehearsal, she finally said yes. I took her to the cheapest bar nearby, the Blarney Stone, and had to admit that I only had enough money for one beer. We split it. So it's safe to say that Leslie wasn't after me for my money.

Right before I was cast in that play, I had broken up with the girlfriend with whom I originally moved to New York. The income gap between us had become a problem, and I had trouble holding up my side of the rent. Ultimately, we wound up on different paths and eventually grew apart.

I moved out of our apartment and moved into a dumpy sublet on the Lower East Side with the guitar player from my college band, Andy York, who had stayed in North Carolina when I moved to New York. I told him he needed to move up here where all the music was happening, that he was too good a player to stay in NC, and we found an apartment together. At the time, I still had some rock-star dreams myself.

We put some music together and performed at coffee houses, open mikes and dive bars. In the end, Andy did alright for himself, as he has been John Mellencamp's lead guitar player since 1994. He was always a great guitarist, and it's been fun to watch his success over the years. I've had a lot of fun telling people he was in my college band! Andy and I roomed together for a few years, right up until Leslie and I got married in 1986 and moved into our own place.

Andy and I found an apartment in Brooklyn, about a forty-five-minute train ride into Manhattan, where I found work, through a temp agency called Proofreaders Unlimited, as a legal proofreader. An actress friend of mine had made a living doing it, and she taught me the skill. In the Reagan economy, business was booming, and law firms were busy. It was possible to work almost as much as I wanted for an hourly wage of between eighteen and twenty-two dollars an hour, depending on the shift. This was good money at the time, and made it possible for us to stay in New York.

The overnight shift paid the most, and it also fit my life-style. I would go into the office at eleven o'clock at night and work until seven or eight the next morning, which made it possible for me to go to auditions during the day. Even when I had a role in a play at night, I'd finish up, then go back to the office and proofread.

My wife, Leslie, also had goals of becoming a full-time actress, and she was fully committed to the idea that this is what we were going to do, and this was the profession we were going to follow. It was great to have a partner who understood the struggle and who had the same passion and vision to achieve the same goals. The apartment where we had to live when we were first married was quite modest—a one-bedroom, four-story walk-up in Hell's Kitchen on Forty-Ninth Street and Eighth Avenue—no elevator, bathtub/shower in the kitchen, no AC, lunatic neighbors, crack smokers on our front stoop, halls that reeked of urine, etc. If the person in the apartment above us spilled a glass of water, it leaked into our living room, and when we flushed our toilet, water leaked into the apartment below us—all for the low, low price of $702 a month. Once, Leslie's sister Stacy came to visit us, and she was a bit shocked. She said to Leslie, "I just couldn't live this way."

To which Leslie replied, "You could. If you had a dream and this was the way to pursue it, you could." (She's just the best!)

From 1984 to 1986, acting gigs were sporadic. I did a little work here and there, mostly low-paying off-Broadway plays, a stupid commercial, and the like. Then, in 1986, I found out it was possible to buy a Screen Actors Guild (SAG) card if you were already a member of Actors' Equity, which, thanks to *Dogs*, I was.

It cost three hundred bucks, which was quite a bit of money to me at the time. But I went ahead and bought my card. I figured I was going to need it if I wanted to do movies and television, which of course I did. It turned out to be one of the best professional decisions I had made up to that point, because when those opportunities started to present themselves, I was already in the union and able to work.

Also in 1986, I was cast in a touring play about Martin Luther King Jr. called *I Have a Dream*, produced by the National Black Touring Circuit headed by the legendary Woodie King Jr., who is still active in the theater. Looking back at it now, being cast in that play really saved me. We would go out on the road for six to eight weeks, traveling around to different cities, and it gave me a chance to make money and have an income while also honing my craft. That show, in my mind, made me a professional actor and prepared me for future opportunities. It was no doubt a huge turning point in my career and my life in general.

In the coming years, I would keep getting cast in plays here and there, but nothing major was happening. The "big break," as all actors dream of having, wasn't happening for me just yet, and more and more the topic of leaving New York would make its way into conversation between Leslie and me. Do we want to stay here? Is it worth it to keep pursuing this dream? What about starting a family? Having a normal life?

The conversation became serious in 1988. Leslie was serious about wanting to leave New York. She had grown tired of the hunt for acting roles, and weary of the grind of proofreading and word processing jobs that we had to do just to pay the rent. At that time I wanted to stay. I wanted to keep pushing. I was starting to get better parts in plays, was doing a one-man show, and was studying with the legendary acting coach Wynn Handman of the American Place Theatre, which he cofounded. Wynn helped shape the careers of everyone from Dustin Hoffman to Richard Gere and many more. I even acted in an off-Broadway play at his theater called *The Unguided Missile*, starring the great Estelle Parsons as Martha Mitchell of Watergate fame.

My one-man show, which I started developing in Wynn's class, was called *Rev. Jimmy Lee Curtis's Hour of Awesome Power*. The premise of the show was that I was a street, preacher in New York City—and they were everywhere then—and for the first time, I had rented a theater so I could preach indoors. I didn't charge admission, but I did take up a collection, while I played the piano and sang Hank Williams' "I Saw the Light." It was very Andy Kaufman-ish. I never broke character, and I didn't advertise my name, just the character's. I did it for three years off and on, took it to England for three weeks, and performed excerpts of it in comedy clubs, where I tried to get people to pour out their alcoholic drinks and follow me into the street to pray. It was a lot of fun, and it made me able to employ myself when no one else was employing me. It gave me hope.

So I felt like I was on the right track and wanted to stay in the city, but Leslie and I were pulling in different directions, and it got to the point where we were having questions about staying together. We seemed to be totally at cross purposes.

Then something happened that put everything in perspective for me. Leslie got pregnant, and the answer to whether we'd stay in New York became clear: we were leaving. Everything completely changed for me. My career no longer seemed so important. There was no way we were going to raise a baby in the jungles of New York in a four-story walk-up, with me making twenty dollars an hour as a proofreader.

I have come to believe over the years that this turn of events was a direct intervention by God. Our becoming expecting parents kept us together during the first dangerous time we had faced in our marriage, and, as you will see, it actually saved my career as well. I believe this was God telling me that I was too focused on less important things, and that simple change in my perspective put me on the path to an acting career—though I had no idea of that at the time.

Now it was back to where I started. Goodbye, New York; hello (again), North Carolina.

CHAPTER 3

FROM GRAVY AND BISCUITS
TO *FRIED GREEN TOMATOES*

When Leslie and I got back to North Carolina, my parents, at that time, owned the Parkway Restaurant, which was a fairly well-known establishment in Sylva, North Carolina. It had been there for thirty years and gained fame and notoriety from the time that Burt Reynolds went on *The Tonight Show* and said it was the worst restaurant he'd ever eaten at.

He was filming *Deliverance*, and they shot a little scene in Sylva, and he went to the Parkway Restaurant to eat. They wouldn't let him brown bag (hide alcohol in a brown paper bag, or BYOB, as they say) because Jackson County was a dry county back then. Obviously, Mr. Reynolds didn't take kindly to that, and that's what he told Johnny Carson that the Parkway was the worst restaurant that he'd ever eaten at. All because they wouldn't let him drink. Thankfully, those comments were made *before* my parents took over the place.

My father was splitting his time between running his accounting business and the restaurant. He suggested that I take over managing the place, which would free him up to focus on his business and take some of the burden off him, and it would also allow Leslie and me to build a little home there and get ready for the birth of our child.

The Parkway was a staple of the community, a meet-and-greet type of place offering daily specials, breakfast, lunch, and dinner. We'd open at 6:00 a.m. and close at 9:30 p.m. Basically, I was supposed to close the restaurant at night, serve on stand-by duty in case an employee didn't show up (which happened a lot), and be a jack-of-all-trades, from dishwashing to manning the grill. Even Leslie would have to come in and wait tables sometimes on days that were super busy. It really was a family affair. I mean, every day there was some form of chaos— Sam the cook would get drunk and not show up, so I'd have to come in at 6:00 a.m. and make the gravy and the biscuits and everything else. But we couldn't fire Sam, because there was no one to replace him! So we just had to live with it. It was quite a chore. And all of this paid me around two hundred dollars a week.

The initial plan when moving back home was to go back to school. Leslie was enrolled in Western Carolina University to get a master's degree, and I thought I'd do the same thing. I had been an English major, so maybe I'd just be a professor. But I wasn't really completely ready to give up on my dream. I had signed on with a talent agency in Charlotte, North Carolina, called the Jan Thompson Agency, or JTA. They thought I had an impressive resume from my years in New York, and they'd send me out for auditions here and there. I was a big fish in a little pond again.

The deal I had with my dad was that I'd manage the restaurant, but if I had an audition, I could go. If I had to tell

Dad that I had to go to Atlanta tomorrow or Charlotte next week, I could do it. I had that freedom.

The auditioning process was crazy. A lot of the auditions were in Wilmington, North Carolina, which was a six-and-a-half-hour drive. I would take off in the morning and leave at 6:00 a.m. to get to Wilmington at about 1 p.m. and do my audition at 1:30 or 2:00. The audition would take about ten minutes, and then I'd just get back in the car and drive home.

Around this time as well, my prolific writer and director friend Mike Bencivenga was making a low-budget feature film called *Losers in Love*. Mike asked me to come back to New York to play a supporting role, but when I read the script, I felt like I was perfect for one of the lead Losers. The script was an homage to the Hope and Crosby *Road to...* movies of the fifties, about two heartbroken men who swore off women forever—only to have to save a damsel in distress on their trip from Florida to New York.

After much begging, insisting, and letter-writing on my part, culminating in a videotaped audition for the role that I mailed to Mike, I finally won him over and landed the role. So, due to budget considerations, I would travel to New York for one weekend a month to shoot for two days and then go back to North Carolina to the restaurant, while Mike raised the money so we could shoot the next month. We did this for eighteen months. While the movie was barely released—although it was a pretty big hit in Poland—this experience probably taught me more about film acting than anything else had up to that point in my life. It gave me confidence when I auditioned for larger productions, because I had so much experience in front of the camera. And I suppose it is a testament to my desire to become an actor. I wanted it so badly that I was willing to do all that traveling—the hours of driving, the flying back and forth, sleeping on couches, anything I had to do—to make it happen.

So there's a lost classic out there for all you crazed Nick Searcy fans to track down: *Losers in Love* (1993).

Back in NC, the very first movie I auditioned for was *Days of Thunder*. It was a pretty good little role, with five or six lines as a highway patrolman. I remember being so nervous when I auditioned for Tony Scott. I generally don't get nervous in auditions, but on this one, I was *really* nervous. I mean, my knees were shaking throughout the whole thing. (Strangely enough, years later, I auditioned for Tony Scott again, and my knees shook again!)

After a few months went by without hearing a word, the agent called and said that I'd gotten the part. Needless to say, I was overjoyed. Finally, my dream was starting to happen.

In the time in between, I had gone on auditions for other things and gotten a couple of day-player roles. I had a one-liner in a movie called *Love Field* and another one-liner in some little TV movie. There were a lot of these little roles that paid SAG day-player rates of about four hundred dollars, which was two weeks of work at the restaurant. It was during these auditions that I made friends with the greatest casting directors in the southeastern United States, Fincannon and Associates. Mark, Craig, and Lisa Mae Fincannon really gave me my start in the business, and I am friends with them to this day.

Love Field was the first major movie I was cast in. Jonathan Kaplan was the director, and I drove to Wilson,

North Carolina, which was a five-hour drive from where we were living. My role in the film was to pull over to the side of the road where Michelle Pfeiffer was hitching and say, "Hop on in." That's it. That was my only line, "Hop on in."

When I auditioned for the job, I walked into the room, introduced myself to Mr. Kaplan, and he said, "All right, let's hear it."

I said, "Okay, here goes." I cleared my throat, paused for a about three seconds, and said, "Hop on in!"

Jonathan Kaplan looked at me and said, "I might want to give you a bigger part."

Later on that week after I got home, Kaplan called my agent and asked if I would come and do the table read for *Love Field*, and read all the other roles with the stars, which I thought was a big honor. I thought, *Great, I get to meet Michelle Pfeiffer, I get to meet Denzel Washington*, who at that time was going play the role of Paul Cater.

I go to read, and I'm supposed to be there to read all the other characters in the script besides Denzel's and Michelle's roles. And *Love Field*, of course, was a story about racism and an interracial couple in 1963 going on a bus to Love Field, which was the airport in Dallas where President Kennedy would arrive before his assassination.

I'm at the table read, which was for some reason at a local private airport, and Denzel had just flown in on a private jet that morning. He'd just finished filming Spike Lee's *Malcolm X*. Now, I'm reading all the racist-cop parts, and all the bad-white-guy parts, and all the horrible words in the script, with many instances of the N-word. And every time I'd say it in the first fifteen to thirty pages, Denzel would say, "Nope.

We're not going to have that." And I'd look at Kaplan, who just looked back at me. And I'm thinking, *What am I supposed to do? Not read what's in the script?* After another few pages and another few bad words, Denzel said, "I want to stop this reading. I want to talk with the director."

Now the room is cleared, and we're all waiting in another room while Denzel talks to Jonathan for about fifteen minutes. Then he walks out of the room, goes back to his plane, and flies away. It was quite shocking, as you might imagine. Then there was some chaos and a bit of a delay, and they wound up casting Dennis Haysbert in the Denzel Washington role and went ahead and made the movie. After that reading, Kaplan ended up giving me a part as an FBI agent, and it was still just one line. I walk up to Michelle Pfeiffer, and I say, "I'm from the FBI. We'd like to talk to you for a few minutes." And that was it.

After *Love Field*, I made the decision that from then on, I'd only audition for mainstream television and film work. I was getting work in industrial-type films, spots for companies and advertisements that paid well but were never going to be bought or shown anywhere for major audiences to see. Even though I only had one line, *Love Field* gave me a taste of the big leagues, and that's where I wanted to be.

The first time I was called to the set of *Days of Thunder*, they were filming in Charlotte. They told me I was part of a cover set, which meant that I was backup. If they weren't able to shoot the scene they were scheduled to shoot, they would still need me there just in case.

At that time, I was doing a play at the community theater in Sylva, North Carolina. I was the lead in a play called *Talk*

Radio, written by Eric Bogosian, which was later adapted into a movie by Oliver Stone starring Bogosian. It's a weird kind of play onstage, where you don't really stand face-to-face with the other character you're interacting with. They're supposed to be on the phone and they're onstage, but you're not looking at them and you don't see them.

About a week before the play started, I was still on the set of *Days of Thunder* waiting for my scene to be filmed, and I told everyone involved with the play that I had to be on the set and wait it out. They were paying me a daily rate for the movie, which was a lot more than I was used to getting, so I had all the actors in the play record their lines on tape so I could listen to their lines and rehearse mine while waiting to shoot my scene.

After about four days, the production team on *Thunder* said they weren't going to get to me just yet, and they sent me packing. I went home and did the play *Talk Radio*, and three weeks later, the production team called me and said, "Okay, we're back in. We're going to shoot the scene in Florence, South Carolina."

I went to Florence, and this time they really were going to shoot that scene. It was finally happening. It was a night shoot, and by the time they got to me, it was three in the morning. We drove out to this location, and of course this was a scene with Robert Duvall, Tom Cruise, John C. Reilly, and Leilani Sarelle.

In the scene, Leilani and I play fake cops that pull over Tom Cruise's racing trailer. I'm knocking on the door and getting everyone to come out onto the street and line up against the trailer, saying that everybody's under arrest, then Leilani comes out and frisks Tom, and opens her shirt to him, and explains that it's all a big trick set up by Duvall's character.

All during that scene, I kept thinking to myself, *Robert Duvall is right in front of me, and I'm actually talking to him!* He was a hero of mine. But besides acting in the scene, there was no real conversation between myself and the other actors. They had been filming all day and were all exhausted. I was later told that there were some legendary blowouts between Duvall and Tony Scott. Unfortunately, I wasn't around to witness them.

However, when we were shooting that scene, there's one particular event that I remember happening. Everyone in the racing trailer had to be lined up and frisked, and Tony Scott had previously worked out beforehand with Leilani that she would actually grab Tom Cruise's crotch, not just fake it. She did it and thought it would be a funny joke and everyone would be laughing. But Tom wasn't expecting it, and he got really upset.

"Why would you do that? Who told you to do that?" Tom said. He didn't think it was funny at all. I don't know why. Maybe he didn't want Leilani going around town saying, "I grabbed Tom Cruise's package, and it wasn't all that great." Who knows?

All in all, working on that film took me to two different locations over a total of about seven days, and we filmed for about two hours for a scene that was maybe two minutes long. They also had somehow violated the SAG rules about dropping an actor and then picking him up later, and so they wound up paying me for all the time in between the two locations! It was quite a lot of money for us at the time. Gotta love the movie business.

When *Days of Thunder* was finally released, it was such a blockbuster that it was basically shown in every theater in the country, including my hometown theater in Sylva, North Carolina. They were so excited to have a hometown boy in the movie that they put "Days of Thunder…with Nick Searcy" on the marquee. It was a funny and exciting moment for me, my family, and my hometown.

By that time, our beautiful daughter, Chloe, had been born, and I was grateful to be making a living doing the thing I loved. Being a big star was no longer at the top of my list of goals or achievements. Being able to feed my family by being a working (and paid) actor was a good enough reward for me. Would it lead to bigger things? I always had hope and luck on my side.

Well, as luck would have it, the Los Angeles-based casting director on *Days of Thunder*, David Rubin, would turn out to be the same casting director a year later on *Fried Green Tomatoes*, and he remembered me and called me in to audition. I actually had a job booked, acting in an in-house industrial film in Raleigh on the same day as the audition, which I canceled. It was a difficult decision, because we needed the money, but *Fried Green Tomatoes* was adapted from a fairly famous book, and I knew that it might be a great movie. So I drove down to Atlanta to read for the part of Sheriff Curtis Smoote, which an actor friend of mine, Raynor Scheine, ended up getting. It was a small, one-scene role, but at that time, that was the kind of part I usually read for.

After I auditioned, the director said, "That was pretty good." Then he turned to the casting director and said, "I'd like to read him for Frank Bennett."

I obviously had no idea who that was, and the Atlanta-based casting director, Shay Griffin, said, "We don't have anyone reading for that part today, so I haven't pulled sides."

And the director, Jon Avnet, said, "I think he might be good for Frank. Let's read him for Frank."

I waited in the lobby until Shay came out and handed me a stack of about fifteen pages, and I thought, *Holy shit! This is a real part!* Not only was it a real part, but I'd get to play a bad guy. So I flipped through the pages, and Shay told me to take as long as I needed to get familiar with the material. I took about an hour before I told them I was ready.

I went back in with material in hand and auditioned for the part of Frank Bennett. I thought it went well, and Jon Avnet said, "Alright. Thanks, that was a good job." I left, and when I didn't hear anything back for a week, I figured I hadn't gotten the part.

Well, they finally called back and said that Jon Avnet wanted to see me again, and would I drive down to Atlanta to audition again? I did, and this happened four more times. Four more times I drove to Atlanta to read for Jon Avnet. After the fourth audition, Avnet said, "Okay. Thanks."

By this time, I'd gotten a little more comfortable being in Avnet's company, and I said, "Why do you keep calling me in? Is there something that you want to see that I'm not doing?"

And he said, "No, I'm just waiting for you to screw up." Jon, as I came to know, had a great, nasty, acerbic wit. My kind of guy. But my hopes by now were sky-high. This was a great role, one that could put me on the map, and the fact that he kept bringing me back again and again HAD to mean something, didn't it? I was certain that I was going to get the part.

Then a few days after the fifth audition, my agent in Charlotte called and said, "Avnet said you did a really good job, but he's not going to give you the part of Frank. He wants to give you another part." That part turned out to be the role of a Klansman on the street during a rally, and it was a one-liner, *and I would be wearing a HOOD.* My face wouldn't even be on screen.

I promptly directed my agent to tell Jon Avnet that he could take that Klansman and stick it up his ass. (I don't think they actually told him that.)

I was heartbroken. I remember that moment—being on vacation with my wife, sitting in the hotel, and breaking down crying. I really thought I was going to get that part. But if it wasn't meant to be, then it wasn't meant to be. I tried to keep my head up, but I was very disappointed. Bad thoughts kept creeping in, like, *Maybe this is as far as you get, pal. Maybe you need to go to grad school after all.*

Then soon after, on a Thursday night, I got a call that Jon Avnet wanted to see me again. The next day, I drove to Atlanta one last time, and they were supposed to start shooting the following Monday. I got there, and they told me I didn't have to read again.

I waited in Avnet's office, and finally he came in, chewing gum or a carrot or something—he always seemed to be chewing on something—and said, "Well, Nick, do you think you're ready to do a part as big as Frank Bennett?"

I felt this incredible stirring in my chest, and I said, "Jon, I've been ready for this for ten years. It was the ten years of struggle that I wasn't ready for."

He laughed, shook my hand, and said, "Alright. Be back on Monday." Inside, I was ready to explode with a combination of joy, relief, and satisfaction that all the hard work and patience and persistence that I had put into this craft was paying off in a big way.

I very calmly responded, "Thank you, Mr. Avnet. I look forward to working with you." I then ran out of that office, got in my father's 1989 cherry-red Corvette that I had borrowed, and burned rubber out of the parking lot. Jon Avnet could see my car from his second-story office window, and he heard me screaming, "Yee-haw" as I peeled out of the parking lot. Now every time he sees me, he tells that story.

I will be forever grateful to Jon Avnet for giving me, an unknown, no-name kid from Cullowhee, North Carolina, the role of the main bad guy in one of the most beloved and iconic films of the last fifty years. Jon actually wound up directing quite a few episodes of *Justified*, and whenever I would see him, I would ask:

"Have they started calling you 'the Man Who Discovered Nick Searcy' yet?"

And with typical Avnet sarcasm, he would reply "Yeah, but they don't mean it as a compliment."

Finally, I was on my way.

CHAPTER 4

I GOT THE PART

The first day I arrived on the set of *Fried Green Tomatoes*, my name wasn't on the call sheet. I did a double take and looked again. Nope. My name still wasn't there. I thought, *Did I actually get this part? What's going on here?* There's literally another actor's name next to the role of Frank Bennett. I went up to the nearest production assistant and asked if I was being pranked.

Thankfully, I was assured it was a mistake. I could breathe again. I think the reason I got the part at the last minute was because the actor before me had wanted too much money, or his schedule didn't work out, and Jon Avnet told me later that he'd been telling people, "It's okay, it's okay, I've got a local guy that can do this part."

The other actor's name on the call sheet was Arliss Howard, whom I ended up working with twenty years later on an episode of *Manhunt: Deadly Games* (again, directed by Jon Avnet!), which was about Eric Rudolph hiding out in the mountains of North Carolina for years after he bombed the 1996 Olympics in Atlanta. I asked him about his name being on the *Fried Green Tomatoes* call sheet, but he said he didn't have any recollection of being offered that part. So, to this day, I don't know why his name was on the call sheet.

I was so grateful to be on that set. Since I was late to the game, I approached everything and everyone with respect and caution. I had a funny exchange early on with Mary-Louise Parker. I was playing her abusive husband in the film. Mary-Louise and I both went to North Carolina School of the Arts. I went for a few semesters before dropping out, and she stuck it out and graduated (of course, she's much younger than me).

So, the first day of shooting, I was doing a pretty big scene with Mary-Louise, Mary Stuart Masterson, and Stan Shaw, and I remember at one point, Mary-Louise was complaining about how long it takes to do films, and she said something to the effect of, "I hate movies. I'd much prefer working onstage."

And I said, without even thinking, "Well, last week I was flipping burgers and frying chicken. So this beats that." She didn't seem to think that was very funny.

The whole experience was really, really eye-opening for me. I learned a lot being there. One of the first things I filmed was me sitting in a truck, and Jon Avnet came over to me and said, "I want you *tabula rasa*. You know what that means? Just look over there and don't put any emotion on your face. I want the audience to read in what you're thinking." He was basically telling me, "Don't look over there like you're mean. Don't look over there like you want to kill somebody. Just look over there." And that was a very important lesson for me. I was nervous, and I was playing the bad guy, and I wanted to be intimidating and all that. But I learned that it's much more intimidating to let the character do what he does—to not put a lot of spin on the character, just let his actions, or lack of actions and emotions, speak for themselves. And that's something I carry with me to this day.

There were actually a few stunts in the film, and they had a stuntman there for me for a very dramatic scene in which I was supposed to throw Mary-Louise over my shoulder and carry her up the stairs. I was so gung-ho that when they asked, "Do you need a stuntman for this?" I said, "No, no, I'm fine. I can carry her." This was a mistake, I quickly learned.

I really wanted to do it myself—until about the fourteenth time that I picked her up, put her over my shoulder, and carried her up the stairs. I learned another very important lesson that day: If you're ever in a movie and they ask you if you need a stuntman, say yes. Because you don't know how many times you're going have to do the same task over and over and over again. If somebody thinks you might need stuntman, trust me, you just might. I've never again refused a stuntman.

That day was a lot of fun. Jon Avnet was having a blast. He set up one shot where I stood on the camera dolly and Mary Stuart Masterson jumped on my back and was supposed to be tearing at my eyes and hitting me. They took that camera dolly and spun it around so that they could get a crazy frenetic shot of the fight. It was the first time I'd really done those kinds of physical stunts where I'm slapping people, kicking people, and punching people, and I learned a lot very quickly about working that way in film.

I've done stage combat, but of course, the rules for film are different. To sell a punch, if the camera is pointed at you and you're punching somebody with his back to the camera, you have to make sure that the camera can see your fist on both sides of his head. That will sell the punch.

A terrifically brutal moment in the film is when my character, Frank Bennett, kicks his wife, Ruth, down the stairs. Avnet gave me a direction that I have never forgotten, and I've used over and over again in my life. He told me, "When you kick her down the stairs, just do it matter-of-factly. Don't try to show us what you're feeling with your face. You're a blank slate. Let your actions speak for themselves, and let the audience read into you. When you turn around and kick her down the stairs, don't act. Just do it." When you see the film, the coldness of that act, the lack of emotion, makes Frank Bennett even more chilling.

Fortunately, I got to meet Jessica Tandy. In *Fried Green Tomatoes* there is a present-day section, and a 1930s section. I was in the '30s section. The present-day section, starring Kathy Bates and Ms. Tandy, was shot first, and there was very little overlap between the two time periods. But there was one day when cast members for the modern section of the film and the thirties section were both on set, and when I got on the bus, I saw Jessica Tandy.

I said, "Hello, Ms. Tandy, I'm Nick Searcy, I just wanted to say hello."

And she said, "Oh, and who do you play, young man?"

I said, "Well, I'm playing Frank."

She said, "Oh, my goodness, the bad guy."

And I said, "Well, I don't know. In the story, my wife's been cheating on me. I think I've got a point here."

Jessica Tandy smiled at me, and she said, "You know, that's the way you have to look at it."

When you're playing a villain, it's important to remember that villains don't think they're villains. They think they're doing the right thing, and that's always something to keep in mind. You shouldn't play "evil," because in your mind, you aren't. You're doing what you think is right, even if it's wrong. Thank you, Ms. Tandy. I have played a lot of bad guys, and I've never forgotten that. Maybe that's why I've played so many!

Mostly, everyone was really gracious to me, with one exception, and that was when I met Cicely Tyson. Cicely was a strictly method actress, and when she came into the makeup trailer one day, I was very excited about meeting her. She was a legend to me. I remembered her from the movie *Sounder*, and we had some mutual friends because I'd done the Martin Luther King Jr. tour with Woodie King Jr. in New York. I said, "Miss Tyson, it's an honor to meet you. I'm Nick Searcy."

I held my hand out, and Cicely Tyson looked at me and said, "I'm not shaking your hand." And she walked on past me.

I looked at the makeup person, and she said, "She's in character." So Cicely Tyson hated my guts because she's in character and I'm the wife-beating, Klansman husband. Cicely would keep that going all the way through the shoot.

When we did the scene in the movie where her character kills my character, she's supposed to hit me in the head with a frying pan. They had this big rubber frying pan that she was to hit me with, and Avnet showed it to me and said, "It's flexible, it's not going to hurt." But when it came time to film the scene, my character doesn't see it coming, and Cicely slapped me in the back of the head with that frying pan so hard that I saw stars! I went down like a ton of bricks and played the scene out, and when Avnet yelled, "Cut," I jump up off the ground and said, "Holy shit! Is she really going to kill me with that thing?"

Jon said, "It's rubber, it's not going to hurt you."

I said, "Well, let me hit you with that thing, and you tell me how it feels." We had to do another two or three takes, and Cicely never backed off. She hit me as hard as she could every time. Cicely Tyson certainly stayed in character.

Looking back, for me, the great thing about being on that set and being around all those legendary actors was that I always felt like I belonged there. I never felt like I couldn't do this. But what was tentative for me, at the start, was learning set etiquette. Up to that point, I really hadn't been involved to the extent where I was playing an actual character who had an arc and a number of different scenes. And it was that experience that was a little nerve-wracking for me, because making a movie is not like making a play. You're doing things all out of sequence, and you have to hear in your head the rest of the symphony while you're just playing your one little part, your one little note. Whereas in a play, you go through it every day, and you plan it out, and you do it in order, and you have more tries at it. With a film, you get three or four tries, and that's about it. It's very rare that you do five, six, or seven takes. So it was a whole new experience, like getting a crash course in how to build a character on film, something I'd never really done before, because it had always been just one scene or one little line that I had to deliver.

After filming, you never know how successful a movie is going to be until it comes out, and you get a reaction from the public. But I had a good feeling about this one, and I was proud of it. I was proud of the work that I'd done. I thought I'd done a good job. I thought I'd been in good shape. Then it was just a matter of going back to work and waiting for the film to come out to see what happens. After *Fried Green Tomatoes*, I got cast in a few TV movies in North Carolina, but the future was still uncertain.

My wife and I had an agreement that whenever she finished getting her master's degree at Western Carolina University, we'd go to California and try to make it out there. When *Fried Green Tomatoes* came along, it gave me a chance to add a significant credit in a major movie to my resume even before I went out to the West Coast. And when the movie was released, they had a big premiere in downtown Atlanta for all the cast and crew. I brought my whole family and some friends. I think I had an entourage of around fifteen people at the premiere. After watching it on the big screen, it became apparent to everybody that this movie was really, really good. So the search was on for an agent in Los Angeles.

I called a friend of mine in New York, and he referred me to a lady named Marilyn Black, who was a manager, not an agent, in Los Angeles, and I called her on his recommendation. She said, "Who are you? I've never heard of you."

And I said, "Well, there's a movie that came out, *Fried Green Tomatoes*, that I have a role in."

She said, "Oh yeah, I've heard of that."

I said, "Well, go see that movie, and if you think you can work with me, then maybe we can make a deal."

Marilyn ended up calling me back a couple of days later and said, "Yeah, I think I can do something with you." And she became my manager for the next ten years.

I flew out to LA to go to a few appointments she had set up for me while I was still living in North Carolina. I was out there for a week or two, and I got an episode of *LA Law*, which was a big, big show. This was at the time when the Rodney King riots hit in 1992, and everything was chaos. They were shooting *LA Law* on the 20th Century Fox lot at night, and you could see all the smoke coming over the mountains from all the riots and all the burning. I said, "You know, there's one shot tomorrow. Do you *really* need me for that shot? If not, I'd really like to get the hell out of here."

They let me go a day early, and I flew back to North Carolina, where I continued to work at my parents' restaurant. Of course, things were a little different after *Fried Green Tomatoes* came out. Someone walked into the place to eat one day and asked the waitress, "Does Nick Searcy ever come back in here now that he's a big star?"

She said, "Yeah, he's in the back cooking your chicken right now." They sent back a napkin for me to autograph, and I sent it back out with the person's chicken dinner.

My success was very surreal. Nobody saw it coming, and for me it was a moment of "I told you I could do this," even though I didn't know that I could do it from the beginning.

I had finally proven to my family—and to myself—that I wasn't crazy, and I could do what I said I was going to do.

A lot of life is being in the right place at the right time. I think it all had to happen the way it did for me. I needed the time in New York to work with Wynn Handman and do all those plays and learn how to act. At the same time, if we had not moved back to North Carolina, I don't think any of it would have happened. We needed to face the true facts of our lives, because it would have been miserable to try to have a baby in New York. In some sense, at that moment when we left New York, there was a feeling in my heart that maybe I was just giving up, maybe I should stay. But the fact is, if I had not moved back to North Carolina and started working in movies that were shot locally, *Fried Green Tomatoes* would never have happened for me, and I wouldn't be here.

Looking back, I believe it was divine intervention. God has really taken care of me. I've been very fortunate. I think a big lesson I learned was that it's always better to make decisions for my family rather than my career. In some sense that helped my career even more, because we were making decisions based on the most important thing.

Before we made the move to California, I landed a few TV and movie roles that were mostly shot in Atlanta, which was an easy two-and-a-half-hour drive for me. I shot an episode of *In the Heat of the Night*, which starred Carroll O'Connor, another hero of mine. I didn't have any scenes with Mr. O'Connor, but I did meet him in the trailer, so that was special. I played the bad guy of the week.

I was cast in a TV movie called *A Mother's Right: The Elizabeth Morgan Story*, and the most interesting thing about that experience was that I got to play the son of Rip Torn. I loved being around him and talking with him. He was just such a great, weird old guy. There's a scene in the film where I'm supposed to be talking with Rip (my father) about my sister, and originally it was set around a dinner table. But we were shooting on a location that had a basketball hoop outside.

I suggested to the director that maybe we could do this scene with Rip Torn and me while shooting baskets, because I knew that he was a basketball player and so was I. The director thought it was a great idea, so we did the scene where we're just shooting hoops in the backyard. I was a really good shooter and hit all my shots, and when we got through the scene, the director said, "Okay, that's great, let's move on," and Rip said, "No, no, wait, wait. We can't move on."

The director asked why, and Rip said, "I missed my shot. I don't want to look like an asshole here." So, we had to keep shooting until Rip made his shot. I really loved working with him. It was great fun to listen to his stories of opening for rock bands at the Fillmore East back in the '60s, of his experiences with Janis Joplin and other icons. And Rip's movie Payday is still one of my personal favorites and a great forgotten classic film. Rip was a national treasure.

In September of 1992, we finally made the long-awaited move to Los Angeles. Leslie had gotten her Master's degree and we were ready to go. After saying goodbye to my parents and Searcy's Restaurant (the name had been changed from the Parkway by then), we took off across I-40 driving our two-seater Uhaul truck. We made a little bed for Chloe, now three, behind the bench front seat, and we were also towing our car, a 1988 Nissan Maxima wagon, and inside the wagon was our dog, Daisy, and our cat, Flower, with the windows cracked so they could breathe. We were definitely the Burbank Hillbillies. We had found a little 2-bedroom rental house in Burbank, a town Leslie and I chose because it was close to some of our good friends. The deposit and first months rent took over HALF of our savings at the time, so there was no time to lose. I had to get to work.

When we landed, Leslie immediately was hired at St. Joseph's hospital to work in the cardiac rehabilitation facility, teaching exercise to recovering heart patients. This allowed me to be Chloe's "Mr. Mom" at home, as well as freeing me up to go to auditions. Sometimes I would take Chloe with me when I auditioned. I remember her being so excited to go with me to and audition for *Free Willy 2*, the sequel to the movie about the whale, but when we got to the office, she was disappointed: "Where's Willy?"

One of the first movies I auditioned for out there was *The Fugitive*. I read to be one of Tommy Lee Jones's US Marshals—and got close, but no cigar. Then they wound up asking me to come in and read for a screen test with some of the other actors, because they were considering other actors before they hired Tommy Lee.

They brought me in to read the train wreck scene, and I read the part of the local Sheriff. I was reading lines with all these different actors, and one of them was Michael Rooker. Because there was some kind of mix-up, Michael didn't come in when he was supposed to. It was two or three hours of waiting, and I didn't know if I should just hang around or leave. I was getting a little restless, but the man who was running the screen test said, "Just relax. You're going to get a part in the movie. Just hang with us."

So I stayed, and the whole thing ended up taking five or six hours when it should have taken one, but they cast me as the sheriff at the train wreck, which was being filmed in my hometown of Sylva, North Carolina. What are the odds of that? I had moved across the entire country six months earlier only to be cast in a movie that would be flying me back to my hometown for work. I'd be shooting for a week, and they asked if I wanted a hotel room. I said, "No, I'll just stay with my parents."

My scene was with Tommy Lee Jones, who, as I mentioned, was one of my inspirations as a kid. We had a read-through the day before shooting the train-wreck scene, because it was a really big scene that had all these important elements. The director, Andy Davis, was there, and so were Tommy Lee Jones and all the other actors. Tommy Lee Jones had a lot of say in how that movie was done. He changed a lot of the script, adapting it to himself, and I think that's why he won the Oscar— he rewrote all his lines and tailored the role to himself. I took that to heart, and over the years, have tried to do that myself—within reason, of course.

After the read-through, Tommy Lee Jones said to me, in front of the entire room, "I don't like the way you're playing that part."

I said, "What do you mean?"

And he said, "I think you're playing him too intelligent. I think you should play him like he's a stupid redneck and he can barely read, and you're just some stupid, small-town-bumpkin sheriff." Well, I didn't want to play the character that way. I had this idea like, I want to show that I can do something other than stupid redneck, because I've been playing a lot of stupid rednecks.

I said, "Mr. Jones, I'm sorry, but I don't really see the character that way. I think he's maybe a good politician and he's pretty well-spoken, but he just doesn't know what he's doing in terms of law enforcement. I think that's a more interesting way to play the character."

Tommy Lee Jones said, "Well, I don't."

I looked over at the director, and Andrew didn't really want to go against Tommy Lee Jones, and he said, "I don't know, Nick, you might think about it."

I finally decided that I was going to stand my ground and play the character the way I saw him. I said, "I'm sorry, Mr. Jones, I just don't see the character that way." It was a fairly tense moment as I knew that I could be fired. But I was old-school theater actor at that point, and in the theater, an actor *never* tells another actor how to act. That is the director's job. And at the time, I just felt like I had to stand up for myself, no matter what. There was a moment of stunned silence in the room. I think Mr. Jones was used to having his way.

Needless to say, after that, Tommy Lee Jones really did not like me. You could say I wasn't his favorite actor on set. During that week of shooting, it was very cold at night, and he would invite a lot of other actors into his huge trailer that had a hot tub and a fireplace. It was like a small village. Needless to say, I never received an invite.

(A similar thing happened to me on the set of another movie I was cast in called *The Real McCoy*, starring Kim Basinger. Kim would come in with basically the whole scene rewritten. And I remember going to the producer of the movie and saying, "You know, this scene was a lot more interesting before. I mean, can't we just go back to the way it was originally written?"

He said, "Look, I have to keep her happy. Her name is worth five million dollars in Europe. Frankly, I don't give a shit what you guys say.")

In *The Fugitive*, when I was doing the scene with Tommy Lee Jones, at the end of it, there's a famous line where I say, "Okay, boys, we're shutting it down. Wyatt Earp is here to mop up for us." It was the last line I had in the script.

When the cameras were rolling, Tommy Lee Jones suddenly improvised and said, "Oh, Wyatt Earp. That's very funny."

My training at the time told me I was supposed to improvise back, and I said, "Well, I'm glad you like it."

Tommy Lee Jones looked at me, and said, very angrily, "You little son of a bitch!"

Now, I didn't know if he was acting or not. I'm thinking, "Is this real or is he improvising?" But the director said, "Cut! Moving on!" and that was it. That was the end of the scene. To this day, I don't know if he was acting or if he was really calling me a son of a bitch. My guess is the latter.

Shortly after the *The Fugitive*, I was cast in the movie *The War*, starring Kevin Costner and Elijah Wood, which gave me a chance to work with Jon Avnet again. It was not a huge role, but he wanted me to be in the movie, so he gave me a part. In the film I'm supposed to be carrying a briefcase up a flight of stairs and knock on the door. When I got up there, I set the briefcase down, and it fell over, and I had to pick it up. This was a little awkward, but we went on with the scene.

After it was over, I said, "Do you want to do that again since I fumbled the briefcase?"

John said, "No! No! I love that. That's a happy accident. We're going to keep that in the film." So, on screen, I actually fumble over my own briefcase, which turned out to be another good lesson from Jon. Always keep going in a take, no matter what happens, until the director says, "Cut." Happy accidents are sometimes the best thing in a film. You may end up using the mistake, which may turn out to be better than what you had planned.

That same year, 1994, I landed a role in the movie *Nell*, starring Jodie Foster. And once again, I found myself filming in the mountains of North Carolina, not far from where I grew up. I was booked for about ten weeks, which was the longest role I'd ever had in a film. We shot that in Fontana Village, which is about forty-five to fifty miles from my home in North Carolina. So, for ten weeks, it was really like being at movie camp.

Every night, Liam Neeson and Natasha Richardson, director Michael Apted, and all the cast and crew would sit around watching the dailies. That was really fun, and I probably learned more about directing doing *Nell* than I did on any other film. Watching the dailies every night with a great director like Michael Apted and a great cinematographer like Dante Spinotti was just a tremendous learning experience for me.

Jodie Foster couldn't have been nicer, and I got along great with Liam Neeson. Most of my scenes were with him, and we had a lot of laughs together. At the end of filming, we gave each other the familiar movie set goodbye: "Oh, let's get together again." No, we never did.

Before filming, Jodie Foster's people floated around a little memo to everyone, basically saying, "Don't bother Jodie, don't try to engage her when she's on the set. What she's doing is very taxing because she's such a strict method actor." I thought, *Well, maybe I shouldn't even look at her,"* but she was always just coming up to the cast and crew and talking. You know that memo obviously came from somebody on her staff who was trying to take care of her; it didn't come from her. She was very personable, and we've almost worked together again a couple of times over the years since she started directing films, but it never worked out. Overall, filming that movie with her and that entire cast and crew was one of my best experiences on set.

Between *Fried Green Tomatoes*, *The Fugitive*, and *Nell*, I now had a few high-profile major motion pictures under my belt, and my agents at the time were trying to keep me on the road of doing primarily feature films only. Well, I had always gone into this business, from the beginning, just to make a living doing it. I've got a family. I can't be so precious and picky and turn down money that would help put food on my family's table. So, against my representation's advice, I was more attracted to venturing into TV than they were.

So, along comes a TV show called *American Gothic*. Marilyn, my manager, sent me the script, and when I read it, I wanted to play the lead. I thought that I'd be good for the evil sheriff role, which Gary Cole ended up playing, with me playing his deputy. Originally, I was not supposed to be in the series. They were supposed to kill me off in the pilot, but they liked my character enough that they completely changed the part and kept me alive.

We shot the pilot, and the series ended up getting picked up. Well, guess where they were shooting the show. Unbelievably, back in North Carolina. By this time, we had been through the Northridge earthquake in 1994, which shook us up both physically and mentally, so we were pretty excited to get out of LA. We'd moved from North Carolina to LA in 1992, and now, in 1995, we were moving back to Wilmington for *American Gothic*. Even though the show lasted only one year (one year of filming that aired over the span of three years), we ended up staying in Wilmington, North Carolina, for the next nine years.

In 1996, I wound up producing and directing a feature film called *Paradise Falls*. A fellow actor from my hometown, Sean Bridgers, who had acted with me in the movie *Nell*, had written a script with his mother, novelist Sue Ellen Bridgers, about two young boys who decide to rob a train to save the family farm in 1934 during the Depression. We raised the money locally and shot the film in our hometown on 35mm film for three hundred thousand dollars, a truly incredible feat.

Paradise Falls won six film festival awards, including Best Feature at the 1998 Hollywood Film Awards, but we never were able to release the film until nearly 25 years later, when we reedited and renamed it *Carolina Low*. It's now available on Amazon Prime. But in 1996, *Clerks* by Kevin Smith, shot on 16mm, was all the rage. The down-and-dirty, indie film look was in, and our film was an homage to John Ford's *The Searchers*, an epic throwback style, totally out of step with the popular fashion of the day. I highly recommend it. It's a little slow-paced by today's standards, but beautifully shot by my good friend Mark Petersen, who has been the director of photography on every film I have directed since. It's a very satisfying story, well-acted and well-told. It also features some great action sequences, a train robbery and a well-choreographed climactic shootout, all against the backdrop of the beautiful Smoky Mountains of North Carolina. I could write an entire book about the experience. Check it out!

I was able to keep my agent and continue to get pretty steady work on the east side of our continent. But I distinctly remember what my agent sarcastically told me when I relayed the news that we were relocating to North Carolina to do the *American Gothic* series: "So you're a *TV* guy now? I thought you were a feature guy?" That was the Hollywood frame of mind back then. Features were king. These days, that way of thinking has totally flipped, and all the money and attention is on television.

It never bothered me to be known as a "TV guy." What's so bad about it? I was supporting my family while doing what I loved for a living. In fact, one of my very next TV gigs after *American Gothic* would end up taking me *From the Earth to the Moon*.

CHAPTER 5

FROM THE EARTH TO THE MOON— AND BACK TO LOS ANGELES

This was a major deal for me. Not only did I land an import- ant role on a prime-time miniseries on HBO, but I'd also a get a chance to work with a great cast of talented actors, including Tom Hanks. I auditioned for the role at the last minute and ended up getting the part of astronaut Deke Slayton. And all of a sudden, I was going to have to be in Orlando, Florida, on and off for about seven months.

I got down there on the first day, and I had recently shaved my head, not knowing that I was going to be playing a guy with a flattop. So the first thing they had to do was construct a wig for me, a full-head wig, so that I could get through the first couple of episodes until my hair grew back out.

An interesting thing about *From the Earth to the Moon* was that when we were filming one of the first episodes, Tony Goldwyn was playing Neil Armstrong, Cary Elwes was playing Michael Collins, and Tom Sizemore was cast to play Buzz Aldrin.

We shot with Sizemore for a couple of days, but I kept thinking to myself that Tom looked a little bit too heavy to be an astronaut. He was definitely too heavy for a flight suit. He talked an awful lot too. There was just something off about him that day. It certainly seemed a little bit weird. After two days of shooting with Sizemore, they let him go, and we ended up reshooting all his scenes with Bryan Cranston.

I think that what happened to Tom Sizemore was that Tom Hanks, a coproducer of the miniseries, pulled him aside and basically said, "You know, this is not going to work out, but I've got something else for you..." I don't know that for a fact, but I suspect something like that happened, because Tom Sizemore went off to England to film *Saving Private Ryan* instead of being too fat in *From the Earth to the Moon*.

It was a real kick to play an astronaut! I had visited Cape Canaveral as a kid and studied the space program in school growing up, so the NASA missions were a big part of my childhood. During filming we shot in the original block-house where they controlled all the Mercury missions, which was a thrill.

Above all else, it was really an honor to play Deke Slayton, just because he was such an interesting character. One of the original Mercury 7 astronauts, Deke wasn't allowed to fly because doctors discovered he had a heart murmur, but he soon became the de facto head of the astronaut corps, selecting who went on each mission. After the moon missions were over, Deke was cleared for spaceflight and in 1975 was the docking module pilot for the US-USSR Apollo-Soyuz Test Project, the first crewed international space mission.

Unfortunately, I never got to meet Deke Slayton, who passed away two years prior to filming. I did talk to his widow, Bobbie, quite a bit while doing research for the role. However, there was no shortage of former astronauts on set. Jim Lovell was there, along with Dave Scott, giving us technical advice. The authenticity of everything was very powerful. Being able to shoot in Orlando and on the Cape was really an educational and wonderful experience.

I also got to work with so many good directors—Peter Berg, Frank Marshall, Lili Fini Zanuck, Jon Turtletaub, and others, and also Graham Yost, who would play a huge role in my career later (There you go Graham, are you happy now?)—and I think I met every thirtysomething character actor in Hollywood. I worked with everybody—Stephen Root, Cary Elwes, Chris Ellis, John Carroll Lynch, Adam Baldwin, and the list goes on and on. I got to be friends with a lot of these great character actors, many of whom I'm still in touch with today.

Working on *From the Earth to the Moon* was the first time I got to meet and work with Tom Hanks. Tom was the producer and directed one episode that I was in. He gave me advice that I'll never forget. It was funny but also really good advice, because it was so simple and so spot-on.

I had a big monologue in the scene he was directing where I had to tell the astronauts which one of them would be flying to the moon. It was a very dramatic scene, with an extreme close-up of me, and we did it in one take. Afterward, Tom came over to me and sat there and thought for a second, then he looked at me and simply said, "Don't move your head so much."

That was quite brilliant, because the close-up shot was what they call a "haircut," tight on my face, so of course I shouldn't be slinging my head around. I've never forgotten that, because that's just really experienced and accurate film-acting advice. He didn't try to get in my head and give me some weird emotional gobbledygook. He gave me technically sound, easy-to-understand direction.

Being a part of that cast was a tremendous experience. The only real drama (if you want to call it that) behind the scenes was when Tom Sizemore had to be replaced. However, I will say this: We were shooting on Disney property and staying in the Disney hotels. I was there for so long that by the end of filming, I was like, "Just get me out of here, please. Put me up in SeaWorld or anywhere else." Why? Because every time I'd get a wake-up call, Mickey Mouse would be on the other end saying, "Good morning! It's a beautiful day in the neighborhood, come out and play with Mickey." And when I'd go downstairs for lunch, Goofy and Snow White would be meandering around. There's only so much of that a man can take.

Right after *From the Earth to the Moon*, I landed a TV series on the UPN network called *Seven Days*, which was a science fiction series that ran for three seasons. The first season shot in Los Angeles, and this is important because it brought me back to LA in 1998.

Leslie and I had moved back to North Carolina from LA when I was cast in *American Gothic*, and now, with my role in UPN's *Seven Days*, we were returning to LA at UPN's expense. We kept our house in Wilmington, though, as we didn't know how long this would last, and we rented a house in our old neighborhood of Burbank.

The first season was shot in LA, and then when the series got picked up for a second season, they moved the whole show to Vancouver, British Columbia. There was no way I wanted to go to Vancouver, so we went back to North Carolina, and I commuted back and forth for seasons two and three of *Seven Days*. Since they'd already relocated me once, I had my agent argue that the show not be allowed to relocate me again by forcing me to move to Vancouver. So they had to accommodate me by confining my character to one location per episode for 90 percent of the episodes, with the exception of a couple of times a season when they wanted to feature my character more extensively.

That was quite a tough two years. It was about a twelve-hour commute for me, door to door, from North Carolina to Vancouver. It was also not a very happy set. All the actors were upset about having to move to Vancouver, and there was some bad blood because of that. While I think *Seven Days* actually turned out to be a fun and inventive series, it was not a pleasure to make, and sadly, it is very hard to find now after the demise of UPN.

It was in between seasons of *Seven Days* that I was cast in a movie called *Tigerland*, directed by Joel Schumacher and starring Colin Farrell. I was cast off of a videotaped audition and brought down to Jacksonville, Florida. Schumacher was a very experienced Hollywood director, and for this particular film he was shooting in what back then was called the Dogme 95 style. It was a 16mm documentary-style way of shooting that was somewhat popular in Europe.

Schumacher shot really down and dirty and fast-paced, with handheld camerawork, and I really loved it. I really liked the pace of it. And I got to work with Colin Farrell for the first time. Schumacher had seen Colin in a play in England and cast him in the lead role in *Tigerland*, which was really the movie that made Colin Farrell a big star.

I got along great with Colin. He was a little bit of a rowdy fellow back then, and I remember having a few drinks with him one night. We were talking, and I told him, "You know, you better get ready. You're going to be very popular when this movie comes out. This is going to make you a star, so you better be ready for all that entails. It's gonna be a lot of craziness and a lot of temptation."

So, of course, he went on to become a big star and partied like crazy, although I think he's calmed down quite a bit these days. He's such a talent, one of the best actors I've ever worked with.

I really enjoyed that whole experience. I remember Joel had a great sense of humor, and there was one day when we were working on a basic-training scene, and he was walking around talking to a bunch of people doing push-ups in the mud saying, "I know it's the army, but does everybody have to be in green all the time? I come from the costume department; can we get a little color here?"

During that time, my wife and I were doing artificial insemination treatments. Leslie would do a home test that would tell her when she was ovulating. When she was, we would have about a three-day window to get to the doctor's office and complete the process. Right in the middle of filming *Tigerland*, she called on a Thursday and told me that the coming weekend was the best time to "do the deed." Of course, I was in Jacksonville and she was still in California.

I went to the producers and said, "Can I just pop home for the weekend?"

They were skeptical. "We don't want to risk it. You have to be here on Monday."

So I went to Joel directly, behind their backs—which I probably should not have done, but Leslie and I were really committed to having another child. I told him what the situation was, and he said, "Oh for God's sake, go home and get your wife pregnant. Be back on Monday."

I really, really loved Joel. He passed away in June 2022 at age eighty. Just a great guy, and I'll always miss him.

After filming *Tigerland*, it was back to work on *Seven Days*, and soon after, the movie *Cast Away* came around. *Cast Away* was unique because my scenes in the film were shot a year and a half apart because we had to shoot scenes with a heavy Tom Hanks and then scenes showing an emaciated Tom after his character had been stranded for years on an uninhabited island. They gave him eighteen months away to lose the weight he had gained.

I shot the first part of my scenes in *Cast Away* in 1999 and the second part in 2000. Having known Tom and working with him on *From the Earth to the Moon* certainly didn't hurt my chances, but I don't think that's the only reason I landed the role of his FedEx friend Stan. Robert Zemeckis was the director, and I remember something he said in the director's commentary on the DVD of *Cast Away*. When I first appeared on the screen. He said, "Yeah, I cast Nick Searcy in that part. I mean, look at the guy; he just looks like a FedEx employee." I'm still not sure if that was a compliment or not.

My first scene in the movie was one long Steadicam shot. Tom Hanks and I were climbing on board the ill-fated cargo jet, and the production team was using other big airplanes for background in the shot. They were like, "Okay, let's move the airplane back, and let's do this again." It was just amazing that they were using jumbo *airplanes* as our extras. I was expecting it to be this really long day of shooting, and when we got there, we shot the scene about eleven times, and then I thought they were going to get more coverage shots. But Zemeckis said, "That's it. Okay, we got it. Everybody's done." He got the scene in one shot. Zemeckis was always very, very prepared and knew exactly what he wanted. He was a real pleasure to work with.

It was a unique experience working with Tom Hanks. He's the kind of actor who has been in this game for so long, and has worked with so many legendary figures, that he has his own style, his own intentions, and he's going to do whatever he wants no matter what you do. At least that was my impression of him.

One of the toughest parts for me about working with Tom was that I'd be in the middle of a scene with him, and I would catch myself watching him rather than staying in the moment. While he was talking in the scene, I'd be thinking, *Well, this is a very different character for Tom. He's usually much more animated*—and then suddenly remembering, *Oh my God, it's my line!* It was distracting in that way. I was so used to watching him and being an audience member and not at all used to interacting with him and exchanging lines on camera.

Soon after *Cast Away* was finished, I got cast in a movie called *One Hour Photo*. It was a small role, but I did get to work with Robin Williams, which was so much fun. What a nice guy he was. He signed pictures for my daughter, who was a big *Mrs. Doubtfire* fan.

We had to shoot overnight on *One Hour Photo*, since we were filming in a functioning store that operated during the day. We shot from 7:00 p.m. to 7:00 a.m. We were near the end of shooting one night, and I was doing a scene but Robin was basically done—he just had to yell something at me from across the room. The production assistant or the director, Mark Romanek, told Robin, "You know, you can go home now. We're just going to do this last little shot with Nick, and it doesn't have to be you. You're off camera and way across the room."

Robin refused to leave. He said, "No, no, no. I'm going to do my off-camera line for Nick."

I'll never forget how much of a professional he was, and I'll never forget how considerate and respectful he was to me even though I was way down the totem pole. Robin Williams didn't have to do that. And now I always do off-camera work no matter what. I'm doing that for Robin. God bless Robin Williams, RIP.

In the meantime, Leslie and my efforts to get pregnant just didn't work, and we both agreed that we did not want to try fertility drugs, or more invasive measures. We were a bit frustrated and sad about that, for a time—but that seeming disappointment led to one of the most unexpected and rewarding stages of our lives.

CHAPTER 6

OMAR

Leslie and I were lying in bed one night in 1999, and she asked, "Why do you want to have another child?" Leslie's pregnancy with Chloe had been quite an ordeal for her, forty hours in labor. So there was some understandable trepidation there, for both of us, about going through that again. But she was certainly willing to try.

I said, "I think Chloe would benefit from growing up with a sibling, for one thing, and for another, I guess I want to have the experience of raising a boy. We raised our beautiful daughter, and I want to see what raising a boy is like."

She said, "Well, there's no guarantee it would be a boy even if we got pregnant. Why don't we just go adopt one?"

Around that time, my daughter came home from elementary school with a bookmark from the child adoption services in North Carolina which said, "Every child needs a home." My daughter handed me the bookmark and said, "Well, they do, you know."

We called the number on the bookmark that Chloe brought us, got involved with the foster care system, and that's how we eventually ended up adopting our son, Omar. It was a team effort.

Omar was born very prematurely. He weighed three pounds, six ounces—really, really small. But we didn't meet Omar until he was fifteen months old.

When we decided that we were going to adopt, we wanted it to be out of the foster care system. We didn't want to go overseas and do all that. We just wanted to adopt a child who needed a home, and to do that in North Carolina, you had to get qualified by the state's Children's Services agency. So we took the foster care training, which was about eight hours of classes over eight weeks. They asked all sorts of hard questions, like, "What kind of a child are you looking for?" Our daughter, Chloe, was eleven at the time, and we thought it might create a weird dynamic for to her to suddenly end up with an older brother. Also, Leslie and I were in our forties, and starting over with a newborn baby didn't seem like it would suit us at our age. We thought a child who was around five or six would be a good fit for our family.

But once you're qualified, no matter what you have asked for, the foster care system will start calling you and ask, "Can you take this child?" Because the need is great and constant, they don't have the luxury of paying much attention to what you said you wanted when a child suddenly needs a placement. They'll just call you up and go, "Hey, we have these two twin girls who are eleven years old. Can you take them?"

Sometimes, we did "respite" for a couple of children. Respite is what they call it when you're a stopgap placement for a child in an emergency situation who needs a temporary place to stay. We did that a couple of times, and it was difficult. I mean, it's hard on everyone involved. It's hard on the child and hard on you because the child knows they're not going to be there for very long. It's a truly heartbreaking situation, and my heart goes out to parents who sign up for it.

Children want to feel attached and want to be loved. They need caring parents, and they want caring parents. We got a call one time and were told, "There's a newborn baby named Elijah that we'd like you to consider."

We weren't really looking for a newborn, but the three of us began to get excited about the idea, talking about cribs and baby beds and the like, so we jumped in the car and went to the hospital to meet him. We were trying to get our heads wrapped around the idea. When we got to the hospital, we discovered that the baby had been born very premature and needed very extensive care, had be fed every two hours, had hernias that needed to be taken care of, etc. They placed little Elijah in Leslie's arms, and I could see how much she and Chloe wanted to take the baby and help him. But I called a timeout, and we had a family conference in another room. I knew caring for Elijah would have been almost a full-time nursing job for my wife, since I was getting ready to go to Utah for five weeks to do a TV movie and she would have to do it alone.

We ended up deciding to say no. We were all sobbing. We weren't the ones to take this on; we just couldn't do it. It was heartbreaking, but in the end, it was absolutely the right thing for us to have done. We kept track of little Elijah through the agency, and learned he was eventually adopted by another family. But by admitting that we were not equipped to take Elijah on, it opened us up for Omar, our beautiful and beloved son, to come into our lives.

When we got the call to meet Omar, he'd been with a foster family for about a year, and that family was moving out of state. Omar couldn't go with that family because parental rights in his case, for whatever reason, had not yet been terminated. (Ironically, since Omar had been born very prematurely as well, his foster mother, a truly saintly lady named Heather, had done for him exactly what we had felt ourselves unable to do for Elijah.)

We went to meet Omar and his foster family. They were very nice people, with a big family that included four other children and little Omar. When I saw Omar for the first time, he was crawling around on the floor in a diaper. His hair looked a bit crazy, matted and even bald in spots, and he had a bit of a lazy eye, so I couldn't be sure if he was looking at me or not. But for me, it was like being hit by a thunderbolt. The minute I laid eyes on him, I knew he was supposed to be with us. I knew in my heart that he was my son.

I believe that's probably the most direct contact with God I've ever had. God was telling me this was meant to be, this was my son. We were there for about an hour, talking to the family about whether we could take Omar (he would be living with us as a foster child since he hadn't yet been cleared for adoption by the state), and at the end of the meeting, Leslie said, "Well, I guess we've got a lot to think about."

I was like, "What? No, no, we don't. Do we? We don't have to think, do we?" I was already so certain than Omar was meant to be with me. And Heather laughed as she showed us out, telling us yes, we probably should think about it.

About a month later, after a few tense moments where the state wanted to place Omar somewhere else, he came to live with us. We thought the adoption would go fairly quickly after that, but it ended up dragging on for three and a half years as we waited for Omar to be cleared.

What kept happening is what often happens in the foster care system: when the child's biological parents start doing a little bit better, the state starts thinking about giving the child back to them. Omar had only lived a couple of weeks with his biological mother before entering foster care, and he'd been with us now for a year and a half. He was three years old by now and had begun talking—and he was calling us Mom and Dad.

There were court hearings where they considered giving Omar back to the biological parents, and those were really terrifying. I didn't have legal standing at the court, but they let the foster parents make a statement. When I was in court, I would say, "You know, he's been with us this long. He calls us his mother and father. He's not a puppy. You can't just put down a bowl of water and some food and think he's gonna be alright. He's emotionally attached to us, and I really think you should consider leaving him with us."

I got to meet the biological parents that way. We had been taking Omar to Children's Services for his supervised court-ordered visitations with his birth parents. They would always be at the hearings, and I would listen to them speak, and they would see me get up and explain why Omar should stay with our family. We never spoke directly, but we got a sense of each other that way. His birth father, also named Omar, came to some of these hearings, even though he did not live with the birth mom anymore. When I saw him for the first time, it was amazing to me how young he was. And our Omar looked exactly like him.

It got to be 2004, and I had landed a series-regular role in a sitcom for ABC called *Rodney*, starring stand-up comedian and country singer Rodney Carrington, that was going to move us back to California from North Carolina. We were afraid that we wouldn't be able to take Omar with us since his parental rights were still not terminated and he was technically a ward of the State of North Carolina. It got to the point where we were having fantasies of just taking off with Omar and becoming fugitives.

At one of the court hearings, which was not really about Omar but about his brother, I saw his mother, and something in my heart kept saying, "Go talk to her." I went up to the woman and introduced myself.

She said, "I know who you are."

I said, "You know, if you will allow Omar to stay with us, if you voluntarily give up your parental rights, we will stay in touch with you, and you'll always know where he is. And he can visit you. If you just let this process go forward and the state terminates your rights, they won't even tell you where he is, and you'll never see him again."

"Can you put that in writing?" she asked.

"No," I said, "I can't put that in writing, but I promise you. I give you my word, we will stay in touch with you. We want Omar to know you and know where he came from. We don't want anything to be a mystery to him."

She said, "Let me think about it." And a few days later, the social worker called us and said the mother had agreed to voluntarily relinquish her parental rights so we could adopt Omar. And we did keep our promise to her. We always made sure to visit Wilmington once or twice a year so that Omar could see his birth family.

We were so happy for about five minutes—until the social worker informed us that we also had to get permission from the birth *father* as well. And that was going to be tough, because, at that time, no one knew where he was. So we were back to twisting in the wind, with our moving date looming on the horizon.

A couple of months later, the social worker called me and said the biological father was in jail. She had spoken to him about the situation, that the mother had relinquished her rights, and I was told that Omar Senior, or Big Omar, as we called him to differentiate, had refused to do the same. She told me, "He said he don't want his son raised by white people, and he don't want you to take him to California so he'll never see him again. And he don't think the state has the right to take away his son, and he wouldn't feel like a man if he didn't fight to keep him."

When you're going through the foster care training, one of the first things they ask you is: "How do you feel about adopting a child of a different race?" There are couples who go into the foster care system who may be waiting for a white child, but there may not be many available. That doesn't happen as often as it does with respect to other ethnicities. We told them from the beginning that we had no problem with adopting a child of a different race, but the social workers were very concerned. They seemed to have a problem with it, not us.

The social worker, at one point, was trying to place Omar with a single, black mother. Omar's current foster mother advocated for us. "What are you talking about?" Heather told the social worker. "You have a loving mother and father here, and you're ready to give him to a single woman with two other foster kids, who is old enough to be his great-grand-mother, just because of race?"

In my opinion, some in the foster care system are more race-conscious than they should be. I remember having a rather heated discussion with one of the social workers about what was best for Omar, and she told me, "You know, we're really tired of having white people like you coming down here and taking our black babies."

I said, "Now wait a minute. Did I push somebody out of the way? I mean, could you show me who it was that we prevented from taking care of this child? We're trying to fill a need here, and you're treating us like we're doing something wrong."

Another factor in all of this is that the state child protective agencies do not prioritize getting these children adopted. The system is designed to keep the kids in the system, as backwards as that may sound. The system, like most government agencies, exists to feed and perpetuate itself. "The best interests of the child" were words we would hear in court, but it certainly never seemed like those interests were a very high priority for the Department of Social Services.

Eventually, Big Omar was located, in the city jail in Wilmington. I asked to visit him to ask him to give me the right to adopt my Omar. We were limited to talking with each other on phones through a glass partition, just like in the movies. I knew going in, because of what the social worker had told me, that he would be distrustful of me at the beginning. And even though he was Omar's biological father, he was only about nineteen years old. He was a kid himself.

Before I went in to talk to him, I prayed for God to give me the words that I needed. I knew this would be my one chance to convince Big Omar that I could be trusted.

They brought him into the visitation area in his orange suit, and I could not help but notice how young he was. From what he had said to the social worker, I knew that he felt helpless and disrespected by the system. So I tried, as best I could, to show him respect and address each of his concerns one by one.

Talking on the phone to him through the glass, I said, "Omar, I know we're white and he's black, and I can't do anything about that. But I promise you. I'm going to teach him his history. I'm going to make sure he does his homework and goes to school. I am going to take care of him. We are going to have to be in California for a while, and I can't change that either. But I promised his birth mom that we would keep him in her life and visit at least once a year, and I make you the same promise. I love him, we all love him, and I give you my word, man to man, that I will take care of your son, if you'll let us adopt him."

Big Omar said to me, "Tell that social worker to come talk to me tomorrow."

And the next day, he agreed to allow us to adopt Omar.

Big Omar told me later that the fact that I had given him some respect made him more inclined to let me adopt, because he felt like the state was taking away his son like he didn't even exist. And to this day, Big Omar writes to me from jail. I think he's going to get out in about three years, and I hope I can help him when he does.

He's been talking to me about helping him plan for what he's going to do when he gets out, wanting to start a business, and that sort of thing. The funny thing my wife always says is, "When we adopted Omar, we didn't just adopt him, we adopted his whole family." And it's been a real blessing. His brother came to live with us for a while, and we visited his mother and other family members. So, Omar has always known his biological family and where he came from, and I think that has helped him become well-adjusted to everything. There's never been any mystery about his past or why he was adopted.

Adopting Omar was without a doubt one of the best decisions my wife and I have ever made. Omar was a gift from God that we could not have seen coming. He was a wonderful kid growing up and has enhanced our lives in so many ways. He was the most valuable player of the Burroughs High School basketball team his senior year, and has become a great young man with a great heart. He's twenty-two years old now, is studying at a film school, and wants to be in the movie business as well. I can't possibly imagine my life without him.

CHAPTER 7

AN INTERNATIONAL FILM
AND TELEVISION STAR AT LAST

In 2001, we were back in North Carolina and had Omar living with us when the tragic events of 9/11 changed all aspects of our lives. For me, everything stopped. The film business was changed forever, and there was very little happening in the months after the attack. I found myself going without work for over a year. Things got to the point where I had to refinance the house. The interest rates were low, and I thought it would provide me with a little bit of a stopgap, which it did for about thirteen months. But it wasn't easy.

Of course, traveling was harder, and as a result, a lot more actors were sending in tapes instead of going on in-person auditions. I remember auditioning for *Head of State* and *Runaway Jury*, and I was cast in both of them on the same day. My agent called me and excitedly said, "You're not going to believe this, but we've got two movies for you, back-to-back." After being out of work for as long as I had been, this was music to my ears.

We shot *Head of State* first, which starred Chris Rock, and up until that point was the first comedy movie I'd been cast in. I was always telling my agents that I really wanted to audition for sitcoms and comedy stuff, and they'd say, "Well, you know people don't see you as being funny. They see you as *American Gothic* and *Cast Away*."

Chris Rock also directed the movie, and we had a great time together. I remember being at the original read-through, and Chris thought it was hilarious that I was living in North Carolina. He said, in that Chris Rock voice, "How do you do that? How do you live in North Carolina and you have a movie career?"

The first scene we filmed together was the big political debate at the end of the movie, and we were sitting there talking, and Chris said, "We really don't have a big argument in this debate. We really should have some kind of a fight."

And I remembered that *Monty Python* contradiction skit that goes, "I'm here for an argument."

"No, you're not."

"Yes, I am."

"No, you're not."

"Yes, I am. Wait a minute. This isn't an argument; you're simply contradicting me."

"No, I'm not."

I suggested that to Chris, and he said, "Let's try it."

And so we did this whole bit that wound up in the movie. It wasn't in the script. We just start improvising and contradicting one another over and over. "Yes, it is," "No, it isn't," and on and on. *Head of State* really gave me the ability to say, "See, I can also do comedy."

Then came *Runaway Jury*, a film adaptation of John Grisham's 1996 novel. One of the stars of the film was Hollywood legend Gene Hackman.

Gene Hackman was my hero, my idol, the actor I wanted to be like. He was one of the actors I would watch as a kid and think, *If he's doing this, maybe someday I could too.* When I first saw him on set, he had an intimidating presence. In fact, I was so intimidated that I was afraid to talk to him. The thing about Gene Hackman is he takes his work very seriously and doesn't like to be approached or talked to much outside of scenes, so it was awkward for a couple of days.

Eventually, he broke the ice himself. Things finally got to be so awkward, he started to talk to me, and we ended up having some fun on the set. There was an intense scene in the film where Gene was supposed to kick a trash can at me, and the can would go flying through the shot. But he didn't want the trash can to hit me, so he said, "Let's plot this out so that we don't hurt Nick when I kick the can." Then he said to me, "Which way are you going to duck, Nick? Are you going to go right or left?"

I said, "I'm going to go left."

He said, "Okay."

So we film the scene, and Hackman, when I went left, led me to the left—and then nailed me in the shoulder with the trash can.

Then the director said, "Cut. Nick, are you alright?"

I went, "Yeah, yeah, I'm fine. It's no big deal."

Then Gene Hackman went to the guy sitting next to him in the scene and said, "Ten bucks!" Trash can victim or not, it was such an honor to work with him. And on the last day, I was able to get up enough courage to go up to Gene and tell him how much I had admired him over the years, and how much his acting had influenced and inspired me. I was able to "get complete" with Mr. Hackman.

After *Runaway Jury*, I got cast in a bunch of throwaway, one-episode roles in shows like *The West Wing, NCIS, Boston Legal, Army Wives*, and the like. And during this time, I was still harping on my agents to get me auditions for comedic films and sitcoms. Then along came *Rodney*, a network sitcom that I landed.

Rodney was based around the life of Rodney Carrington, who is a very successful singer and stand-up comedian, but mainly only in the middle of the country. He's a very personable cowboy, rodeo, heartland comedian, and his comedy show was absolutely hilarious, but also very blue and very raunchy. The ABC network cleaned him up and put him on television, and we survived for a great two seasons. I played a character named Barry, who was based on Rodney's best friend who had passed away just before the show started. This part on *Rodney* would take us back to California, and ABC would pay for the move, so we decided at that point to just sell everything in North Carolina and move lock, stock, and barrel back to California. Until then, we'd had a house in both places.

During my stint on *Rodney*, I discovered that doing a sitcom is the cushiest possible job for an actor. What a great schedule. We do a read-through on Monday, which took about an hour, and then Rodney and I would go play golf while the writers rewrote the show. We'd go in and work for about two hours on Tuesday, and Rodney and I would go play golf again. And then the writers would make more adjustments, and we'd work for maybe four hours on Wednesday. Best schedule ever.

On Thursday, they'll do all the pre-shoots, which is just filming bits they can't do in front of a live audience. And then on Friday, you go in, and you do a twenty-two-minute play in front of a live audience. It all takes about two and a half hours, and you're done. It's a lot of fun.

You just can't beat that schedule. I was home all the time. We shot the show at the Radford Lot at CBS Studio Center, which is maybe four miles from my house. I could ride my bicycle to work if I wanted to. It was so convenient. I wish it could have gone on forever. Rodney is still one of my dearest friends. He even let me come out and try stand-up comedy, back during COVID when there was nothing to do. I did it with him off and on, filling in when he needed me, for about a year. I consider it a gift that Rodney gave me, letting me get up there onstage and see how it felt. I'll never forget it. Rodney was another one of God's many gifts to me.

Of course, it would have been nice to immediately jump on another sitcom once *Rodney*'s run ended, but sometimes you have to take the work that's in front of you and do the things that come up. I was fortunate in that having done a sitcom, I now had a track record in both comedy and drama.

I shot a couple of horror movies in between seasons of *Rodney* called *Cold Storage* and *Timber Falls*, the latter of which was shot in Romania.

After *Rodney*, I hit a little bit of a drought until 2009, when I was cast in a movie called *The Ugly Truth*, a comedy starring Katherine Heigl and Gerard Butler. I think because

I'd been on *Rodney* and in *Head of State*, the producers were comfortable casting me in this comedy.

I had a really good relationship with Katherine, and I found her to be very professional. For whatever reason, and I don't know why, she had a lot of skin problems, a lot of acne, and spent a lot of time in the makeup trailer, but I found her to be a lot of fun to work with. And I had a really good time with Gerard Butler; he and I got along very well. That whole experience was a lot of fun for me. Also, it was filmed in Los Angeles, so again, I got to be close to home.

Right after *The Ugly Truth*, I got cast in a TV series called *Easy Money*, which shot in Albuquerque, New Mexico. Laurie Metcalf and I played a *nouveau riche* husband and wife who owned a string of payday loan stores and had more money than brains. Jeff Hephner and Jay R. Ferguson played our sons. It was just a terrific show that should have run for years. But it was an unworkable business model. The company that made that show just bought the time slot on the WB network. They bought a single night every week of the run, and they provided the programming.

They were going to sell advertising, but they started selling too late in the season, so our sponsors were like ShamWow and other as-seen-on-TV products. They couldn't get the big sponsors to advertise, so their business model just didn't work. They didn't make enough money, so I think we only did eight episodes out of a twelve-episode guarantee, which was a shame, because it was such an honor to work with Laurie Metcalf.

I was always a fan of Laurie, even going back to the old days when I first moved to New York. One of the very first dates Leslie and I had in New York was an off-Broadway Steppenwolf production of *Balm in Gilead*, and we just loved Laurie's performance, way before she became famous. Getting the chance to work with her was phenomenal.

I quickly picked up a one-episode role on a popular TV series called *The Mentalist*, and then three episodes on another TV series called *Svetlana*, which my friend Iris Bahr created, directed, and starred in. She's a really smart, really funny show creator from Israel. She and I became friends, and *Svetlana* was basically an improvised show about a Russian madam who managed a stable of prostitutes. I played a rival pimp, which was quite fun. She and I had a good time together. I wasn't really getting paid that much for these little gigs with friends, but I liked the people involved in the projects and did them for fun. To be honest, I never thought I would make any money acting anyway, so when I started making pretty good money, it was really unexpected. I became an actor because it was the only thing I wanted to do. I certainly didn't do it because I thought I'd get rich. So I usually don't mind doing projects for love and not money. (Unless everybody's getting paid. Then I want some!)

In 2011, I auditioned for the film *Moneyball* for the major scout part, which I didn't get. But my agent at the time, Joe Rice, called and said, "They want you to be one of the scouts that's just sitting in the room, evaluating the players."

I said, "That sounds like being an extra. I don't think I want to do that." Joe called to tell them that I'd passed, but then he called me again. "They say there's going to be more to it than what's in the script, and they really want you to do it. So, what would you do it for?"

I thought about it and told Joe that if they paid me my daily rate, which no one had paid me in about ten years, then I'd do it. In Hollywood, there used to be these things called "quotes," essentially how much money it would take to get an actor to accept a part. Veteran actors would work their way up to until they were making fifteen thousand dollars a week or so. You'd have a day rate and a weekly rate. Well, none of those things matter anymore. They actually passed a law in California that an employer cannot ask you what you made on your last job, which is the craziest thing, and it threw all these quotes out the window.

But anyway, I said, "Okay, what the hell? If they'll pay me my day rate, I'll do the job." They agreed, and it was a pretty substantial amount. Not a bad deal. I arrived on set to what was supposed to be a three-day job, and we shot for three days with the script as it was. In the scene, six of us were actors, and six of us were real scouts.

After the three-day shoot, Bennett Miller, the director, came in and said that he didn't like anything that we'd done, and we should throw out the script, and that we were going to improvise the whole scene.

Well, at that point, Brad Pitt got mad and left; he just left the set, and he didn't come back for three days. So for three days, they just kept calling us in and letting us sit there and wait, in case Brad Pitt came back to work.

Brad eventually came back to the set, and we did three days of improvising the scene. It was a strange mix among the actors and real scouts. The scouts couldn't act, and the actors were all acting their asses off but didn't know anything about baseball. I didn't mind the delay at all. It turned out to be nine days of work at my day rate, one of the biggest paychecks I ever got.

I found Bennett Miller to be very uncommunicative. The director would never say hello to us or say anything much at all. He treated us like we were all props or pieces of furniture. So I can imagine it wasn't necessarily a pleasant experience to work with him every single day, as Brad Pitt had to do.

The whole time we were shooting *Moneyball*, I was thinking, *What a piece of garbage this is. This movie is going to be awful.* I remember telling my agent, "I don't know what this guy Miller is doing. This is going to be terrible."

And when we were told that we were going to improvise everything the last three days of shooting, I told my agent, "They're paying me the same rate no matter what I do, so I'm just going to sit here and not say anything." And for most of the time, I just sat there and dipped snuff. Then at some point during the third day, I remembered that I'd read the book *Moneyball* while preparing for the role, and there was a line that I thought was funny. We ended up using this bit in the movie. In the scene, one of the scouts is talking about a player and says, "He's got an ugly girlfriend." Another scout responds, "What does that mean?" And I reply, "That guy has no confidence."

I think it's the only line I have in the whole movie. But it was such a funny line that it made the trailer for the film. And I think they even showed it at the Oscars during previews for Best Picture.

I took my son, Omar, to the theater to see the film, which came out in 2011, and when we heard the line, "That guy has no confidence," the audience laughed. Omar turned to me and whispered, "Good job, Dad. You got the first laugh."

In 2012, I worked with my daughter, Chloe, on a web series called *Chloe + Zoë*. My daughter had come home from Yale, and she had been doing some writing and acting with her friend Zoe. They came up with the show concept, which was very funny, and it got written up as one of the best webisode series of the year. They sold a pilot of it to MTV, which never got produced, but they got paid to write it anyway. It's described as two beautiful young women with the personalities of two grumpy old men who are best friends, and it's them against the world. They have a blast slacking off, making fun of everyone, and alienating anyone who likes them.

It's a very funny show that is still up on YouTube. I think there are about twenty episodes, and I'm in about five of them. But again, it was just something I did for fun to work with my talented daughter. She also inspired me to do my own webseries later, *Acting School with Nick Searcy*.

Also in 2012, I did a brief stint on a TV show called *Hot in Cleveland*, starring the legendary Betty White, Jane Leeves, Wendie Malick, and Valerie Bertinelli. Some of the writers on *Hot in Cleveland* had worked on the sitcom *Rodney*, so they brought me in to do two episodes in which I played the warden and Betty White had to go to prison.

Working with another legend like Betty White was an honor, and it was so much fun because I remember when we were doing a rehearsal, I made Betty crack up. We were doing a scene where I was a prison warden and I had to "wand" her to let her into the prison, and she had so much metal in her body that the alarm kept going off. She laughed at something I did (which I can't remember exactly what), but I will always be very proud that I made Betty White laugh. This was another significant moment for me, because one of the main reasons that I wanted to be an actor was when I was a kid watching *The Mary Tyler Moore Show*, and I was looking at the people in that sitcom having fun, I knew I wanted to be like one of those people.

Working with Betty White felt like I had finally come full circle, to have been able to work with some of my heroes, which is the same thing I felt about working on *Runaway Jury* with Gene Hackman.

A funny thing about working on the two episodes of *Hot in Cleveland* was that I played two different characters in two different seasons, Chief Barker and Warden Burkhalter. I think the writers thought it would be funny for me to appear as two different characters. The only difference in appearance was that I wore a mustache as one of them.

Then, along came the big one. The role I'll probably be most remembered for is, of course, Art Mullen in *Justified*.

CHAPTER 8

THE YEARS OF JUSTIFICATION

The way it came about was all because of Graham Yost. He was the showrunner, and I had worked with Graham fifteen years earlier on *From the Earth to the Moon*. We'd gotten along really well, and ever since that time, for fifteen years, I'd email him saying, "I thought we were friends. You're doing all this great stuff, and you never call me," and so on. (Of course you know all this because Graham told you all about it in his typically self-aggrandizing foreword to this book.)

I'd been pestering him, in a joking way, every time I heard that he had a new show. "Hey, congratulations on *Boomtown*. Why haven't I gotten my call time? Why am I not in this?" So when *Justified* came along, Graham told me that when he saw the role of Art Mullen, he thought, *Okay, maybe NOW I can get Nick off my back.*

I did audition for it, but only once, and they cast me off the tape. We shot the pilot in Pittsburgh, because of tax reasons, as usual. The show starred Timothy Olyphant, and he told the FX network that he didn't want to do the show unless it was being shot in Los Angeles, because he had small kids and he didn't want to be away from them. That worked out great for me. We shot it at Santa Clarita Studios in Valencia, which was about a twenty-five-minute drive from Burbank, where I lived. For once, I didn't have to relocate!

It was a dream job. I probably worked twenty days a year, and we'd do thirteen episodes a season. I did that for six years.

My character would be heavy, and by heavy, I mean working more than three days in a couple of episodes, whereas in most of the other episodes I would only work one day. It would mostly just be me in the office, yelling at Raylan for something. So it was a really pleasant job, and I got to work with that great cast—Timothy, Joelle Carter, Walton Goggins, Jacob Pitts—with whom I had a tremendous amount of fun. Jacob and I liked singing bad harmony in between takes. Our favorite song to butcher was "One," by Three Dog Night.

A lot of those people I'd known from before. I had done a crazy movie with Joelle Carter called *Cold Storage* in 2005, and I knew Walton just because we both got our start in the Southeast. So every day on set was like going to work with friends. I felt like I knew everybody, and Graham knew how to write for me.

In the first season, we did a lot of improvising, and it drove the writers crazy at first, but then they started to catch on that we were enhancing the material and not damaging it. There were a couple of times in the first season when we would get a write-up, and the critics would talk about how good the dialogue was between Raylan and Art in the office. They quoted some lines that we made up that weren't in the script. And I was getting on Graham about that, too, jokingly saying, "You need to give me a credit as a writer, because—obviously—I'm making up the best lines." (But again, you know this already, because Graham told you about it in his foreword. He's trolling me in my own book.)

In season 1, Timothy Olyphant's character, Raylan Givens, kept shooting people. The line I improvised was, "You know, Raylan, if you were in the first grade, and on the first day you bit somebody, and then on the third day you bit somebody else, and on the fourth day you bit somebody else, pretty soon, they would start thinking of you as a biter." This line was quoted many times as an example of the great writing on the show. (I never let Graham forget that.)

I based Art on my own father, James Searcy—his way of sizing people up, his decisiveness, his confidence, his sarcasm, his hilariously dry sense of humor—and most importantly, his unwillingness to ever give up on anything or back down. So whenever anyone tells me how much they loved the character of Art Mullen, I get a very warm feeling—because I know what they are really loving about him is my real father. It's my tribute to him.

This was one also of the first times my politics were known on set. However, it wasn't a major issue. We'd mostly joke about it. They all knew where I was coming from, and I knew where they were coming from. They knew I didn't vote for Obama. I might have been the only actor any of them had ever met who hadn't.

I remember on the pilot I got into a little scrap, or maybe what you'd call a funny discussion, with Tim Olyphant. It was around the time when, I think, David Letterman had made some joke about baseball player Alex Rodriguez having sex with Sarah Palin's daughter, and Sarah Palin came out publicly to voice her disdain for the joke. Tim made some crack about it, and I said, "Oh, come on, now. You know if David Letterman had made that joke about your daughter, you'd feel the same way." Everyone on the set was shocked that someone had stepped up to defend Sarah Palin of all people! That just wasn't done! But that set the tone for everyone going forward. It jokingly became, like, alright, let's not bring up politics around Nick, because he's *crazy*! Timothy and I would continue to have fun discussions here and there, but never anything unpleasant.

At one point, one of the producers said something to me about how Sen. Barbara Boxer (America's second dumbest Senator at the time, second only to Joe Biden, who held the title for 40 years), was retiring, and we all needed to work together to elect another Democrat Senator! I politely told her, "I don't think I'm going to be any help to you in that venture." This is typical on Hollywood sets. Hollywood Democrats never even think that it might be possible that there might be someone on set that isn't a faithful Democrat voter. This producer just assumed that I was "one of them."

I remember that Timothy's dad was a rancher who had lived on the border of Arizona and Mexico. He was also a Green Beret, and he had visited the set during the first season. Olyphant said to me, "My dad wants to meet you." His name was John, but everyone called him Bev, Bev Olyphant.

When I shook his hand, he said, "You know, Tim's told me a lot about you. I think you and I are going to get along fine." So it was fun knowing that Tim's dad was a little bit more on my side of the fence when it came to politics.

One morning when I came to the set, I was listening to Rush Limbaugh on my phone—something that I, like every real, red-blooded American, did every day from noon to 3:00 p.m. Eastern Standard Time. I'd stuck the phone in my pocket, and while we were doing the scene, somehow the bustle as I walked triggered the Rush 24/7 app and Rush's voice began blasting out on the *Justified* set. Olyphant laughed as I tried to turn it off and said, "Now we've got Rush Limbaugh in the show!"

And I turned to him and said, "Wait a minute. How do you know Rush's Voice? ARE YOU A DITTO HEAD?"

Ironically, Rush was a fan of the show, and he talked about it often on the air. One day he mentioned me by name, saying that Art was one of his favorite characters, and I wound up being interviewed on the air by Rush for about twelve minutes—longer, I bragged to everybody, than he talked to Dick Cheney! The *Justified* writers listened to my segment, and then actually wrote in a scene, in season 5, where Art Mullen is sitting in a car, on a stakeout, listening to Rush Limbaugh on the radio. I told Rush I was proud to say that was the only time in television history that a good-guy character was portrayed as a Rush Limbaugh fan.

The one scene of mine that most people remember fondly is the "slow chase" scene in the episode called "Blaze of Glory," where Art Mullen tracks down Frank Reasoner, the character played by Scott Wilson, at the airport as he's trying to escape with a bunch of money. Reasoner has an oxygen tank because he has emphysema, and Art Mullen has bad knees. He tells Reasoner not to run or he'll shoot the oxygen tank: "You remember that scene in *Jaws*?" Reasoner dumps the tank and runs, and Art has to chase him. Reasoner runs out of breath before he gets to the plane, and Art limps up with the oxygen tank, disarms him, gives him the breathing tube, and takes a big dip of snuff. "Well, I bet you wished you'd quit smoking now," he says. "That shit'll kill you." Truly great stuff. (And by the way, I improvised the snuff and the snuff line, Graham. Pay me!)

That scene was directed by my old friend Jon Avnet, and I remember calling him and asking if we could really make a big deal out of that scene, and he did. He laid dolly track down and shot it like a high-speed chase scene. What made it hilarious was that it was just two old-ass crippled men trying to run. On one critic's top-ten list of the best *Justified* scenes, it was number ONE. If I had to pick one scene to show somebody who Art Mullen was in *Justified*, that's the one I would pick.

During season 5, Graham called to tell me that Art Mullen was going to be seriously wounded at the end of that season, and he wanted to reassure me that I was not being killed off, that I would survive for season 6—which was very kind of him (or maybe he just didn't want more nasty emails). But he also said they were going to bring Art's wife onto the show as a character, to nurse me back to health.

At the beginning of season 1, I had been asked to bring in pictures of my family to use as set dressing for my character's office. I filled the room with pictures of Leslie and me, Chloe, and Omar, just in case this kind of situation occurred. I wanted the pictures to establish my real family as Art's family.

I told Graham, "Great! You know she's already cast, right? My wife Leslie's picture has been all over the set for five seasons. Internet nerds will go INSANE if you don't cast the woman in all the pictures as Art's wife!"

Graham said, "Can she act?"

"Graham," I said, "come on. I wouldn't marry a woman who couldn't act."

So Leslie came on board for two episodes as Leslie Mullen, Art Mullen's wife. And she was terrific, as always. Jon Avnet directed the episodes she was in, and ever since he's been needling me: "She's the Searcy with the talent."

As I said, I wouldn't marry a woman who couldn't act.

I had a six-year contract to appear on *Justified*, and I think it was somewhere around the end of the fifth season or the beginning of the sixth when Elmore Leonard passed away. Elmore was a legendary writer and penned the novella *Fire in the Hole*, which *Justified* was based on.

The producers and Tim had made the decision that they were going to make the sixth season the last. They didn't want to go beyond that. I think they were feeling a little bit of creative burnout, and the fact that Elmore Leonard passed away was a big factor.

I think the network was in agreement. It would have cost FX a lot of money to go beyond six seasons, because when you have a six-year contract with actors, and you go beyond that contract, you have to renegotiate with everybody. I think they looked at the situation and assessed that going past the sixth season would cost them too much money and that the best business decision would be to just end the show and move on to create something else.

JUSTIFY THIS

The success of *Justified* has become what I am most known for, and I'm very proud of that. The success of that show was not just due to a grand combination of great writing and great acting, but because they trusted us enough with our characters to give us freedom to improvise and to participate in the creation of the show. Many times, shows are very rigid about sticking to the lines absolutely as written. Another factor was that the show was set in Kentucky, and most law-enforcement shows are set in urban environments. *Justified* depicted the South, not in a stereotypical way, but in a real way. We weren't a bunch of cliché-ridden, stupid rednecks, as is so often the case in Hollywood. The criminals were smart, and the marshals were too. It made it feel real to the audience.

And the humor of the show was such an important factor. Men and women in law enforcement have to deal with some of the most horrible situations you can imagine—murder, domestic violence, car accidents, etc.—and in order to live with that, many times they adopt a sort of gallows humor. That, to me, was one of the things that made *Justified* such a hit with law enforcement types: we were able to put that dark sense of humor into the show, and the truth of it was recognized.

During the last season of *Justified*, I started doing my own web series, inspired by my daughter Chloe's experience with *Chloe + Zoë*, called *Acting School with Nick Searcy*. My filmmaker friend Chris Burgard and I made ten episodes of the show, which basically consists of me making fun of Hollywood stars and ridiculing the entitled Hollywood culture and the trappings of stardom. Olyphant appeared in one of them, and a lot of the show was filmed on the *Justified* lot. For example, I did an entire episode about having a parking space with my name on it, and how proud I was of that, which devolved into a fistfight between myself and Purple Heart recipient Bryan Anderson, an amazing American hero introduced to me by Gary Sinise. It's one of the funniest things I have ever done, and the episode is still available on YouTube.

Graham Yost appears in the series finale, called "The End Time," an epic fifteen-minute episode featuring, among other things, my going into the *Justified* writer's room with my female bodyguards, who slap all the writers around while I bitch about what they wrote for my character. Graham then calls me into his office and shows me in my contract that I am not able to do any other series while I am doing *Justified*. Graham's performance was fantastic in this episode, which ends with a huge musical number. I highly encourage you to watch it, if you've never seen it.

Graham was a good sport to do that, as were all the other writers, and by the end we were a family. I made life-long friends from that show in Graham Yost and Tim Olyphant, Michael Dinner, and the other actors. Although, come to think of it, Graham hasn't cast me in anything since. I'm going to have to start pestering him again.

▓ CHAPTER 9 ▓

LIFE AFTER *JUSTIFIED*

After *Justified*, I was cast in the final episode of *Key & Peele*, the popular sketch comedy series on Comedy Central. A friend of mine worked on the show and told me they needed a cop, and Keegan-Michael Key and Jordan Peele had apparently watched *Justified*, so they were excited about me coming to play the part. It was an episode called "Negrotown," which was a big musical production, and a rather brave, controversial takeoff on police brutality towards black people. Only Key and Peele could have done that and gotten away with it. It's one of the funniest bits I've ever been a part of.

At this point, I had played so many cops and sheriffs that I was starting to feel like I was being typecast into only those roles.

If you're not the leading man in a movie or TV show, if you're not the guy who kisses the girl, you're either the villain or you're the cop. I remember at one point telling my agents that I didn't want to play any more sheriffs unless the show was called *The Sheriff*. But at the same time, I've made a good living in this business playing an awful lot of police officers, military people, marshals, FBI agents, etc. But I've also played an awful lot of villains too. I have played serial killers, rapists, racists, Klansmen, sexual harassers, thieves—I mean, let's face it, I've played a *lot* of Democrats. I'm not proud of it, but somebody's got to do it.

Right after *Justified* ended, I was approached to direct the movie *Gosnell*. While we were putting together that deal, I said, "Yes, I'll direct it, but we have to work on the script. We have to rewrite it and make a shooting script out of it."

So we got the script in shape, set up a shooting schedule, and were gearing up to go to Oklahoma City to shoot *Gosnell* when I got an offer to do *11.22.63*, a miniseries for Hulu based on the Stephen King novel about a teacher who discovers a time portal that leads to October 21, 1960. This teacher goes on a quest to try and prevent the assassination of President John F. Kennedy, which is complicated by the presence of Lee Harvey Oswald and the fact that the teacher is falling in love with the past itself.

I'd always been a big fan of Stephen King and had never gotten a chance to do any of his shows or movies, so I said yes to the miniseries and was really excited about doing it. Now I had to tell everyone involved with *Gosnell* that I was still going to direct the movie but that they had to let me do the miniseries too. They understood my situation and agreed, and I was off to Toronto to film *11.22.63*.

The miniseries starred James Franco and Sarah Gadon, a Canadian actress I really enjoyed working with. Most of my scenes were with James, and he and I had a really close mutual friend named Mark Patrick Gleason. Mark worked with James on his very first film when he was just starting out, and I had worked with Mark on *Justified*. Coincidentally, Mark is now one of my longest-lasting and best friends. So Franco and I talked about him quite a bit, but other than that, we didn't talk much. Franco was very quiet and didn't hang around the set a lot when he wasn't working.

11.22.63 checked my actor's bucket list box for having done a Stephen King project. I had auditioned for Mr. King himself a few times over the years, so it was satisfying to finally score. But as soon as filming was wrapped up, I flew from Toronto straight to Oklahoma City to direct *Gosnell* (which I'll go into greater detail about later in the book). Back-to-back projects. It was a busy time.

Cut to about a year later. I found myself just sitting around and not working much at all. I was starting to get worried. I thought, *Maybe this is it. Did* Gosnell *finish me off now that I'm a known conservative? Maybe this is the end of road for old Nick.*

I remember I was on vacation when I got an email out of nowhere from Guillermo del Toro, basically just flat-out asking me to be in his new movie, *The Shape of Water*. I didn't even have to audition. He was a fan of *11.22.63*, and he was a fan of *Justified*. He was just coming off of doing a series with FX, which is why he was familiar with *Justified*, and that's why he offered me the role, which was incredible.

I was on set shooting for three weeks, and watching del Toro work was a pleasure. He's really a lovely man, and a very thorough and particular director. I remember that he didn't like the traditional military uniform options that the costume shop in Los Angeles presented, so he had a custom uniform made for me. The story was supposed to be a historical fable set during the cold war, but because del Toro hated that particular style of uniform, he had them make up an entirely new one.

Guillermo was also a very actor-friendly director. I was supposed to do a play right after I finished shooting the movie, and *Shape* wound up going a couple of days over. I had to call the play's producers and tell them that I was going to be late, and they said, "Well, you can be a few days late, but you've got to be here by then, or we're going to have to recast the role."

It was a play that I really wanted to do called *Billy & Ray*, written by my friend Mike Bencivenga, about Billy Wilder and Raymond Chandler, and I was to play Raymond Chandler. It's about them writing the movie *Double Indemnity* together. It was a very funny play, and I just loved it. So, I went to Guillermo and said, "You know, I love being here, and I love doing this movie, but I want to do this play, and they need me there by Friday."

Guillermo said, "I will shoot you out so that you can go do your play. I know what it's like to be an actor." And so, he pulled an all-nighter with me. He kept the crew there for like eighteen hours straight and shot all my scenes out so that I could make my flight. I raced to the airport from the set of *The Shape of Water*, got on the plane, and as soon as we landed went straight to rehearsal for the play in Laguna Beach, California. It was a hell of a long day. Needless to say, del Toro didn't have to do that for me. And I'll forever be grateful to him.

I don't think anyone at the time knew just how successful *The Shape of Water* would turn out to be. I mean, I thought it was going to be good, and I liked the script. I'd always been a fan of old horror movies, and I thought this was an interesting throwback to that genre—but it didn't seem like the type of movie that would be an Oscar contender.

It surprised everyone, winning four Oscars at the 2018 Academy Awards, including Best Picture and Best Director for Guillermo del Toro.

As the movie gods would have it, I was in *two* films nominated for Best Picture at the Academy Awards that year, *The Shape of Water* and *Three Billboards Outside Ebbing, Missouri*.

Three Billboards was shot in my hometown, Sylva, North Carolina—just like *The Fugitive*, and my film, *Carolina Low*. I didn't hear anything about the movie until it was close to start of production, and the way I heard of it was that my mother called me up and said, "You know, they're shooting this movie here in town. You should see if you can get in it."

I said, "What's it called?"

And she said, "*Three Billboards* or something."

So I called my agent at the time and said, "They're shooting a movie in my hometown, and it's something called *Three Billboards*."

My agent said, "Yeah, that's a really big movie. That's Martin McDonagh, Sam Rockwell, Woody Harrelson, Frances McDormand. It's a classy project."

I said, "Well, they're filming it in my hometown, and that's the same place where they shot *The Fugitive*, and the same place where I shot *Paradise Falls* [now *Carolina Low*]. Now, I don't know if the producers are aware of it, but there's a local ordinance that says you can't make a movie in Sylva, North Carolina, that Nick Searcy is not in."

My agent said, "Really?"

And I said, "Yep, you better call them up and tell them." (Of course, that wasn't true, but they didn't know that. They were from Hollywood!)

Anyway, my agent called them, and they said, "Well, we have most of our cast already, but we've got two little parts that are left, and if Nick wants to do one, that'd be fine."

So I said, "Sure." If nothing else, it'd be a good reason to go back home and visit my parents.

They said, "There's a dentist who Frances McDormand gets mad at and drills a hole in his hand, and then there's a priest who Frances McDormand gets mad at and cusses out."

I said, "I'll take the priest." I figured I'd rather get cussed out than have a hole drilled in me.

But that's how it came about. I was there for about a week, and one day a man named Phillip, whom I'd known in high school, saw me in a local brewery and came over and said, "Hey, Nick, I have to tell you a funny story about that woman that's doing that movie you're in."

I said, "You mean Frances McDormand?"

Phillip owned this famous little coffee shop in the downtown area that had been there since the '50s, and he said that one morning Francis McDormand walked in. He didn't know who she was and just thought she was another customer. The restaurant was full, and she was looking around, not knowing where to sit. Phillip was at one of the front tables, and he said, "Ma'am, if you're looking for a place to sit, you're welcome to sit down here with me."

She said, "Okay, well, thanks."

Frances sat down and Phillip said, "So, what brings you to town?"

And she said, "Oh, I'm working here."

"Oh, great! What kind of work are you doing?"

She said, "I'm working on the movie."

"Oh, that's great," he said. "It's very exciting to have a movie being filmed here. What do you do on the movie?"

Frances looked at him a little funny and said, "Well, I'm one of the actors."

Philip, still clueless, said, "Well, how exciting. Good for you. Do you have a big part?"

Frances, laughing a little, replied, "I'm pretty much the lead character."

And he said, "Oh, my goodness, good for you! That's great. That must be very exciting!"

Francis McDormand looked at Phillip. "Are you...pulling my leg? You know, I've won an Oscar. Did you ever see the movie *Fargo*?"

Philip said, "No, I never saw that. But good for you. That's great!"

That's my hometown people for you. They just don't really know who these Hollywood people are, and they don't much really care, but they're very nice about it. And so, when I did my scene with Frances, I said, "I have to verify this story with you..."

I ran it back for her, and she said, "Yeah, that's pretty much exactly what happened." Frances thought it was very funny and said it was one of the things she loved about my town. She was a lovely person to work with.

After *Three Billboards*, I found myself in another work drought. I picked up a one-episode part on an NBC show called *Chicago Med*, which had the same writers as *Easy Money*, and they offered me the role. I filmed that episode in Chicago during the winter, which we now know, thanks to Jussie Smollett, is "MAGA Country."

But it was definitely a slow period in my career. I was starting to think something was going on behind the scenes, with me being a known conservative in this business. There was an instance where I read for and landed a role in a Mark Wahlberg-produced show called *Shooter*, which was on the USA network. They gave me the shooting dates, and I was fitted by the costume department, but then over the weekend, I got a call from the production saying, "Never mind. You've been recast."

That was very fishy. I never found out exactly why I was recast, but it was somebody, at the network or somewhere, who must have said, "No. Not that guy."

I was starting to feel like there was something creepy going on. There were parts in TV shows and movies that I used to get and would normally be doing, but now I wasn't even hearing about them. I thought, *Either I've forgotten how to act, and I'm no longer any good, or I'm being penalized for not being a Democrat. It's one or the other.* What was happening? Was I becoming another victim of the left-wing Hollywood mob? Was I being canceled without knowing I was being canceled?

▓ CHAPTER 10 ▓

POINT OF NO RETURN

Hollywood has had a tinge of politics injected into its bloodstream for many decades. But I don't think things have ever been as divided, as contentious, or as heated as they are today. I think we have already crossed the point of no return.

Believe it or not, there was a time when an actor's political beliefs wouldn't be a factor in determining whether or not you got a role. I know it seems like a million years ago, but that time definitely existed. I lived through it in the eighties and most of the nineties.

I started to notice things moving toward the place we find ourselves today around the year 2000, during the Bush-Gore election that was so contested, or maybe even a little before that, during the 1998 Clinton impeachment. That was when Hollywood really started getting its hair on fire, and left-wing actors started to be more public about where they stood politically. Up until that point, I had spent my career mostly in North Carolina, and I knew a lot of actors who had political beliefs on both sides, Republican and Democrat, and we were able to talk openly about politics and joke about it. So when I came to Hollywood in 1992, I didn't really know that it was bad policy to openly be a Republican. I never thought that I should hide my political beliefs. (You might say I was a bit naïve.)

Even during 1995 and 2000, when I was working on *From the Earth to the Moon* and *Cast Away* with Tom Hanks (a well-known liberal and supporter of left-wing causes, and one of the first big-name actors to openly support Barack Obama during his 2008 presidential run), politics never came up. I've never had a discussion with Tom Hanks about politics, and that's the way it should be. But the Left was becoming bolder and more vicious, in every walk of life but especially in Hollywood.

I remember in 2004, when George W. Bush was reelected, I was a regular on the ABC sitcom *Rodney*. We had a table read the morning after the election, and except for Rodney Carrington and me, everyone was pretty unhappy about John F-ing Kerry (who served in Vietnam, as Rush always said) losing the election. In fact, you might say they were distraught and just trying to get through the day. One of the actresses at the table said that she was so upset about the election that she'd held her head out the window while driving to work that day and screamed, "I wish someone would assassinate that man!"

There was a bit of a stunned silence, and I said, "You know, that's…kind of illegal."

But when Obama got elected in 2008, that's when things got completely out of hand. The prevailing attitude became, "If you don't support Obama, you're a racist! How could you not support the first black man to be elected president?"

That's when the situation got really dark. The simmering flame of intolerance toward anyone who disagreed with the Left flared into an inferno during the Obama years.

During that time, it was so bad to be conservative and/or Republican in Los Angeles that Gary Sinise and other conservative actors started a group called Friends of Abe. FOA, as we called it, was basically a top-secret organization for conservatives who couldn't publicly speak their mind. It had reached the point where many of us thought that we'd better keep our mouths shut or the Obama fanatics would never hire us again. The fact of the matter was that you could really hurt your career if you didn't openly support Barack Obama.

And when Donald Trump won the presidency in 2016, all hell broke loose. The liberals weren't hiding it anymore. It basically became an open policy in Hollywood: they were flat-out not going to hire Trump supporters.

Personally, I have never been quiet about my political beliefs. There may have been times when I just didn't say anything, but I've also never hidden anything. The notion to simply remain quiet and keep my head down has never been a natural instinct of mine. But a big turning point for me was when Andrew Breitbart died in 2011, because he died so suddenly and so unexpectedly at the age of forty-three. Andrew was at the first FOA luncheon I ever attended, and his fearlessness, boldness, and brash sense of humor was an inspiration to us all.

When Breitbart died, I said to myself, "What am I waiting for? Why would I ever keep my mouth shut? I don't know how much time I have left. None of us do. What's happening to the country is important to me. I care about my family, and I care about my country, so I'm not going to be silent."

And that's when I went all out on Twitter and started kicking some leftist ass, and I'm still at it today. I refuse to allow these people, who I often refer to as "segments in the Human Democrat Centipede," to bully me into silence, and I encourage you to do the same. Because if they silence you by making you afraid to speak your mind, they have won.

That's when I began questioning the secrecy aspect of Friends of Abe. I felt we needed to stop having secret meetings and, in effect, giving the liberals in our business the power to silence us. We had to stop being afraid of the bullies—because the only way to stop bullies is by standing up to them. Ultimately, I think that's part of why Friends of Abe fell apart. There was a real push by members like me to stop hiding like we were ashamed of what we believed in and to start fighting back.

It's not like there aren't high-profile conservatives in this business; they're just few and far between. You probably already know the bigger names, people like James Woods, Kelsey Grammer, Gary Sinise, and Clint Eastwood. But these are actors with such well-established careers that they don't have to hide their political beliefs, even in today's climate. If your name can get a movie made, you can be as open about your politics as you wish to be.

I know a lot of guys who may not be household names to the general public, but they're probably as famous, even a little more famous, than I am. Many of these people will come up to me and say, "You know, I really admire what you're doing, and I agree with everything you say, but I would never do that, because I know it would crush my career." These are actors you would definitely know, by face if not by name.

The nature of being a conservative in Hollywood is that we don't treat liberals the way they treat us. We've gotten along with crazy liberals for years; we've worked with them, and we've been pleasant to them. When I make a movie, I don't say, "I'm not hiring so-and-so because of their politics," and I don't know any conservative who does. We hire people because they're right for the part. So, lots of times when there's a "conservative" movie, we still hire some liberals. That's one of the biggest differences between us. We can tolerate them—and in fact, we've *had* to tolerate them, since they have us outnumbered—but they can't tolerate us. Like most leftists, they cannot argue their positions sensibly, so their only tactic is to silence you, to bully you into shutting up.

And perhaps the best example of liberal tolerance in Hollywood can be found in my experience with the one and only Sean Penn.

THE TIME I TOLD SEAN PENN WHERE TO PUT HIS OSCAR

I was always a great admirer of Sean Penn's work as an actor. One of the first films I saw him in was *Bad Boys*, during my early days in New York, and there were so many other great performances through the years, including *The Falcon and the Snowman* and one of my favorite films, *At Close Range*, with the great Christopher Walken. I wound up being cast in Sean Penn's 2001 film *The Pledge* and participated in the table read with the entire cast, including Jack Nicholson and Mickey Rourke, among others. Ultimately, I was unable to do the film, because it was shot in Canada and there was at that time a rule that a significant percentage of the cast had to be Canadian citizens, so my character had to played by someone else. But it was great to meet Sean, and we actually had some correspondence—he asked to see the film I directed, *Carolina Low*, and sent me a very nice letter about it. I wouldn't call us friends, but at least we were colleagues.

So I was very excited to be cast opposite him in the 2004 film *The Assassination of Richard Nixon*. I had two very good, meaty scenes with Sean that I thoroughly enjoyed. At that time, of course, Sean was very vocal about being anti-war, anti-Bush, and against the Iraq War—funny how he's now so pro-war in Ukraine, isn't it? But I digress... I wasn't there to debate him, so his politics never came up. To this day, I really love the scenes I did with him, and consider them some of my best work.

But a few months later, out of the blue, I got a very hostile email from Penn. Apparently the wheels were set in motion by a separate email exchange I had with an actress, who shall remain nameless, who told me she was working on an article about "conservatives in Hollywood." She wanted to know what my experience had been like with Sean on *Assassination*.

She seemed a bit disappointed when I told her that we didn't talk politics, as I rarely ever do on a movie set, and that I enjoyed acting with him very much, and we got along just fine. I think she was looking for some red meat, and I wasn't able to supply it. But shortly thereafter, I got another email from this lady, telling me she was "fed up with the bullies in Hollywood" and that she had abandoned the article but had taken it upon herself to send the comments I'd made to "several people in the industry," including Sean Penn.

I felt a bit betrayed, since she seemed to have misrepresented herself to me, and to this day, I still don't know if she was legitimately writing an article, or if the whole thing was a setup so she could "out" me or something. I didn't worry about it too much. I thought I'd been quite gracious —even, dare I say, "tolerant"—in what I said about Sean.

That's when the email came from Penn, in essence telling me to go fuck myself and asking me why I even agreed to work with him if I disagreed with his politics.

I was a bit shocked and, honestly, a bit hurt by it. I tried to respond graciously, saying the truth: that I was there to work as an actor and not to debate him or confront him while he was trying to execute a rather demanding role in a movie. I told him again that I'd enjoyed working with him because, politics aside, I genuinely liked him and respected him as an artist.

Penn's response was even nastier, filled with f-bombs. The part I remember most—I no longer have the email, darn it— is that he said, "What makes you think I give a damn about your so-called RESPECT?"

Well, that made me mad. So I let him have it.

I said, in effect, "All right, buddy, let's get something straight. If I only worked with people in Hollywood who agreed with me, I'd go broke pretty fast. I don't know if you remember this about acting—or if you ever knew, since you were born to a famous Hollywood director—but a lot of us don't have the luxury of choosing roles based on external factors like politics. Sometimes we take roles because we need the money or we need the credit. You see, I don't get a few million dollars every time I grow a mustache or put a perm in my hair, like you do. Acting on screen with you was a great credit for me, and that's why I took the role, and frankly, I don't give a damn what you think about the Iraq War or anything else, for that matter, because you don't know what you're talking about."

Yeah, I was pretty mad. This was a couple weeks after Sean Penn had won an Oscar for *Mystic River*, for God's sakes. I mean, what the hell? Doesn't he have anything better to do than write me shitty emails?

So, in closing, I congratulated him. "Congratulations on your Oscar," I said. "Now do me a favor. Shine it up real nice, put it in your right hand, hold it behind your back as far as you can—and cram that thing up your ass, so you can see it every morning when you wake up, since that's where your head is."

Strangely enough, I haven't worked with Sean Penn again. But I have heard from him. A few years later, I was talking to a famous friend who had worked with Sean about something totally unrelated, and he said to me, "Oh, by the way, Sean Penn told me to give you a message."

I laughed and said, "Oh really? What did he say?"

My friend, who had no idea that I'd suggested what Sean could do with his Oscar, replied, "He told me to tell you he thought you were really good in *The Dead Girl*."

So maybe Sean has forgotten about it all. Who knows? Maybe leftists *can* forgive, after all. But as you can see, it's like I said: we tolerate them, but they can't tolerate us.

So, have I been denied work because of my political beliefs? I'm pretty sure that's happened a couple of times, but it's not something I can prove. The leftists won't tell you that your conservative politics is why you didn't get the job, and they would never say that in public.

But with what's been happening the past three years with the COVID vaccination bullshit, they don't have to. They can do it with your "vaccination status."

They can tell your politics by how you feel about the vaccine. If you say, "I want a religious exemption because I'm not taking the vaccine," the leftists will just cross you off the "acceptable" list right then and there. And they're doing this not just in Hollywood but in almost every institution in the country, including the military. They're kicking all these guys out of the armed forces because they won't take the vaccine. And that's what the Left *always* does, in any country where they gain enough power.

The Left purges everybody who doesn't agree with them, and the vaccination status is the perfect way for them to do it. The projection that the left wing shames the right wing with would be laughable if it weren't so tragic. They call us "Nazis" when they are the real "fascists." Hollywood's leftists have always blacklisted those they want to silence; they just change the reasons why. The government didn't blacklist anyone during the McCarthy era. It was the Hollywood studios that chose to do that. This town has a long history of using politics to ruin people's careers and destroy their lives.

I definitely have not worked in Hollywood as much in the last five or six years as I did before. Part of the reason is because I'm older now, and part of the reason is the woke movement. They don't want old white guys on the screen unless they're playing the bad guy.

I've been asked many times: Why are so many actors or people in the arts associated with liberalism? I think a lot of it is because the nature of being an actor is that you have to empathize with another person—you're trying to understand what they're going through and all that—and that leads to this touchy-feely way of looking at things. It's also a fact that the bad guys in movies and the bad guys in fiction often don't suffer any real consequences—because their actions aren't real.

When you play a murderer, a serial killer (which is what I played in *The Dead Girl*), a rapist, or whatever, you're not actually killing, you're not actually raping. It's all pretend, and there are no real victims like in the real world. So now you can spend your time thinking about how this murderer really was just an abused child, and how it's not really his fault, and he's the real victim. Just like Jessica Tandy told me about Frank Bennett: "That's the way you have to look at it, you know?" Simply put, bad guys don't think they're bad.

But in real life, evil does exist, and it has consequences for the victims and the perpetrators.

I think there's also a kind of herd mentality. The theater is a very insular world, and it's so hard to make a living in it that you risk everything by disagreeing with people about big issues. I don't think a lot of actors really think about these things philosophically. They're just trying to fit in, and they care more about becoming a working actor and becoming successful in their art form than they do about politics. However, on the flip side, people in more reality-based professions—engineers, physicists, and architects, for example—have a different mindset than an artist or an actor.

Actors are even more radicalized these days due to the woke movement, which is a plague that has not only taken over the entertainment industry but also almost every other institution in our country. Hollywood has become the Left's narrative pusher—and not just for the US government. Hollywood is also heavily influenced by Chinese money. The leftist film moguls are so beholden to the Chinese audience, which is such a big market for them, that they really are targeting their movies more toward China than they are toward America.

And we're not just seeing this in the entertainment industry. In July of last year, I was filming something in a little town in Oklahoma that used to be bustling but was now run down and had no industry. I asked a local guy, "Well, what are people doing with all these buildings?" And he told me that the Chinese government had bought a lot of the buildings and was using them to make marijuana.

There's a big market for marijuana now that several states have decriminalized the drug. The Chinese are literally making drugs to get America high. They're working against us in every possible way. And now they're also buying up a lot of farmland with the intention of going after our food supply. This is a very dangerous time. The Left has, in effect, given our country over to people who hate it, and they have been doing so for the better part of the last hundred years.

This outright attack on our institutions and the poisoning of American minds has been going on since at least the 1950s. The education system and entertainment industry are really the big villains in our society today. They have indoctrinated our children with the idea that America is an evil, racist country founded by selfish, greedy, colonizing, land- and slave-owning white people; that the greatest threat to our country is white supremacy; that everything is racist; etc. The education system with its left-wing policies has poisoned entire generations. Kids in public schools right now are intentionally being taught to hate America.

Make no mistake about it, members of the Left in this country are nothing but global socialists, and what they all really want is a one-world government. They want everybody on the same level, except the elites, who get to distribute the money. The biggest obstacle to the global socialist movement is a country founded on individual liberty—and that's America. And there is absolutely no doubt they are here to destroy it.

The global socialists cannot "coexist" with America. They can't have people making their own choices and deciding for themselves what is a good idea or a bad idea. They don't want people thinking for themselves and saying, "I'm going to make this life decision for myself because I think it will benefit me and my family." They can't handle that. They can't control that. So they have to destroy individual liberty. They have to take away freedom.

America is the last country on earth that features and promotes individual liberty, the last country on earth that is based on a bottom-up system of governance that is of, by, and for the people. The left-wing, anti-American, global socialists have been very successful at rolling back our freedoms, whether by claiming systemic racism, or climate change, or pandemics, or whatever scheme they come up with to take away our right to decide for ourselves. We are living in an increasingly totalitarian, socialist state. The question now is: Are we going to get our liberty back? And how?

Granted, not every Democrat is some sort of diabolical socialist. Many of them are just clueless and don't understand what is happening to the country. However, the Democratic Party does a great job of getting people to pay attention to emotional issues and instinctively react to what feels right rather than using their brains to logically think things through. The media tries to make you hate conservatives so much that you must be a bad person—a right-wing Nazi insurrectionist white supremacist domestic terrorist—if you vote for one! And many people are susceptible to that kind of brow-beating pressure.

Every election cycle, all you'll hear from the Left is, "The big bad Republicans are going to take your abortions away." Or, "We Democrats are going to pay off your student loans, and the Republicans won't." Or, "Republicans are burning books." That's also why they pit the races against each other. "They're going to put y'all back in chains!" then-Vice President Biden declared at a 2012 campaign stop; the quote would resurface during the run-up to the 2020 election.

They'll call us "anti-gay" and say all Republicans hate homosexuals, want to force women to stay in the kitchen where they belong and have babies, blah-blah-blah. And frankly, this tactic has given godless people—people without a meaningful higher power—a way to feel morally superior to others without having to humble themselves before the Creator of the universe. They define their goodness, their morality, by how they vote. They have replaced the worship of God with the worship of government—which, by the way, is what communist nations *always* do.

Citizens of this country who actually still love it and want to fight for it must recognize and confront this movement looking to bring us down. It might be too late, but we at least have to try. You have to realize that the leftists want you dead if you dare to oppose them. That may sound like hyperbole, but that statement is backed up by history. In every nation that has become a totalitarian, socialist state, murders and purges on a massive scale have occurred. This is deliberately no longer taught in our schools, because the global socialists want it to happen again.

And we are in an even more dangerous time now, because, as my good friend Evan Sayet puts it, with censorship in social media being what it is, they don't even have to go to the trouble of actually murdering you, disposing of your body, etc. All that can be very tedious and messy. Now they can just ERASE you—remove you from Twitter and Facebook, call you "disinformation," take away your platform on which to express your opinion, cancel you, get you fired from your job because of your opinion—and completely neutralize and silence you—without even having to waste a bullet on you.

If the Left continues to gain more and more power, American will become a totalitarian, socialist state. The best way to combat the Left's increasing power is not through politics—we have to fight them through culture. We have to make feature films and television shows, not just documentaries. Because that is how people are changed: not with facts, but with emotion. And that's what led me to direct *Gosnell*.

CHAPTER 11

GOSNELL

In 2015, I was still working on *Justified* when I was approached by producers Ann McElhinney and Phelim McAleer. I had known Ann and Phelim from Friends of Abe and was familiar with their work from a documentary they produced called *FrackNation*. They asked if I'd be willing to do a short promotional video to help raise funds for a new documentary they wanted to produce about an infamous serial killer and abortion doctor named Kermit Gosnell.

Without hesitation, I said, "Sure. Absolutely. I'll help you fundraise." Besides the fact that I thought this was an important story that the greater public should be aware of, I also wanted to help Ann and Phelim. I knew them as fellow conservatives trying to navigate the choppy waters of liberal Hollywood. I thought part of the strength of having a group like Friends of Abe was to help each other get projects produced that otherwise would never have made it through the front door of any traditional Hollywood studio.

The video I made for the GoFundMe campaign was promptly taken down by the fundraising platform for being "too controversial." Big surprise there, huh? We moved over to Indiegogo, where we started to find some success. I even went on Bill O'Reilly's show on Fox News to help spread the word. It was a very funny appearance, because Bill kept saying, "Well, you know, the critics are going to attack you, saying you're exploiting human suffering."

To which I jokingly replied, "Bill, it's not like we're making *The Human Centipede* here." (I don't think Bill got the reference. He obviously didn't follow me on Twitter!)

Eventually, Ann and Phelim reached their fundraising goal of around $2.3 or $2.4 million. I remember celebrating with them over a few drinks and reminding them that they were now faced with the hardest part of the process: making the movie.

They commissioned Andrew Klavan to write the script. When the time came to look for a director, they reached out and asked for my opinion. I sent them a couple of names that I thought might be inclined to do it, directors I've previously worked with. One of them I knew secretly was a conservative, but I don't want to reveal his name because he's still operating under the radar.

Ann and Phelim ended up meeting with him, and for one reason or another, it just didn't work out. Then they came to me again asking if I knew of anyone else, and I said, "Well, you know, I directed a movie a few years ago. Would you have any interest in seeing it?" They were immediately interested, and I gave them a copy of *Carolina Low* (originally *Paradise Falls*). It's a Robin Hood tale of a family's North Carolina farm that's about to be taken over by the banks during the Depression, and two boys who decide to start robbing those banks and return the money to the people.

After they watched it, I got the call asking if I'd be interested in directing their movie. I said, "Sure, but let me see the script," figuring that if it was a script I could live with, I'd direct. They sent it over, and it was very well written by Andrew Klavan, but there was a problem I found unsolvable.

As I understood it, the producers had asked Andrew to write a script about a journalist who experienced the Gosnell case and had a change of heart and became a pro-life activist, someone who started out pro-choice and became pro-life. I think that may have been the producer's personal journey. But the main storyline was about a fictional reporter who worked at a fictional news network. This, in my view, was a big mistake.

I went to them and said, "Look, I don't think you can do the film this way, because you're going to get killed in the press. What are they already planning to say about this movie? They're going to say you made it all up because you're 'anti-choice.' Now you're giving them the ammunition to make those claims by making the main storyline fictional. And they will be right when they say you made it all up, because you made up this whole character and you didn't focus on the facts of the story."

I said, "What you need to do is throw out the main storyline and tell the story of the attorneys who found out what this man did and convicted him. Just the facts. Just tell the truth about what Gosnell did, how they found him, and how they convicted him." After some discussion, they agreed.

For about the next two months, Ann McElhinney, Phelim McAleer, Magdalena Segeida, and John Sullivan (the other producer), and I sat around in a room, rewriting the script—making it into a functional shooting script as well as changing it from a fictional storyline to a factual and dramatic retelling of exactly what Gosnell did and what his trial was like.

Subsequently, the movie wound up being subtitled: *The Trial of America's Biggest Serial Killer*, because that's what we needed it to be. We needed to tell the truth and not give the critics ammunition by making this a fictional storyline.

The opportunity to direct *Gosnell* came along at a perfect time. I had grown tired of just being an actor for hire. I wanted to start developing my own projects about things that I was interested in. I was coming off my sixth year on a series, and in financial terms, you could say I was pretty flush. I thought this could finally be a move toward making my own films. At the time, I looked at it more as a creative enterprise than a way to make a political statement. As I've always said about these kinds of conservative films: the first thing you have to do is make them *good* movies. Because if you make a piece of crap that wears its politics on its sleeve, and everybody can see it coming a mile away, it's not going be effective in any way. And that's what's wrong with the other side's movies.

Making a *good* movie is fairly subjective. I think what comprises a *good* movie is basically a story that is structurally well told. I know that sounds pretty basic, but so many times people get caught up in the details or the message their movie is supposed to convey. Any time you get caught up in that, you're going to make a less than stellar film.

I think you present the story and let people decide what they think about it rather than trying to tell them what to think. To me, story is *everything*.

I knew directing *Gosnell* was going to be a big step for me. And I knew I was going way out on a limb politically, further than I'd ever been before. I talked to Jon Avnet about it. He read the script and said, "I gotta ask you, why do you want to do this film?"

I said, "Well, I think it's a worthy story that people need to hear, and there's information in the script that I didn't know, about what an abortion procedure really is. And I think everybody needs to know those details. Whatever side of the issue you're on, you should know exactly what it is you're talking about."

When we finally got the script to where we wanted it, I showed it to some really mainstream industry people. The first casting directors I tried to get the producers to hire was a team called Bialy/Thomas, two of the top casting directors in Hollywood. Sharon Bialy and Sherry Thomas have been friends of mine for a long time, and when they read the script, they were willing to come on board. I was overjoyed.

They said, "Yeah, this is a pro-life film, but we think this is a fair treatment of this story, and we think it could be really good." I felt that having them on board would be a huge step forward for us, as they were powerful in mainstream Hollywood. I felt like they would give us credibility, even among the Hollywood crowd. Having their stamp on our project would be invaluable. They're the kind of casting directors that actors do favors for because they know they're going to be doing so many more great things down the line.

Unfortunately, the producers didn't put as much value on that as I did, so we wound up not using them, which, I will admit, was very difficult for me to take and caused a bit of friction.

Looking back, I think going in I was naïve. I thought we had a script that treated the subject fairly and that people on both sides of the question would be able to watch and learn from. I considered what Gosnell had done to be obviously criminal, and at the very least we could all agree on *that*, right? We could agree that when you induce birth and then kill the baby after it's been born, that it's…um, what's the word? BAD! So yeah, going in I was naïve about what the reaction would be. Turns out they would not treat the subject as fairly I thought they would.

Needless to say, there was a delay in the casting process. Nobody wanted to do the film. Everybody was afraid. We were making offers to people who would immediately say: "NO!" We were also trying to get people that we couldn't get. The producers had stars in their eyes, like maybe they could get Mark Wahlberg. And I was like, "Okay, call me back when you get Mark Wahlberg."

I talked to many actors and actresses, and I don't want to say their names because I don't want to damage them, but people who are very high profile. They said flat out they didn't want to participate in the production because they thought it would harm their career. At the time, I remember thinking, *Why are we even bothering with the secret organization of conservatives if you guys are just never going to stand up and do what you think is right?*

It's a problem. There are a lot more conservatives in Hollywood than the general public knows about. There are people you would know by name who literally said to me, "I agree with what you're doing, I agree with what you're saying, but I can't publicly go along with it because I know that it would affect my ability to feed my family."

I figured it was time to stand up. I've always said it's one thing to admit there's a leftist bias in Hollywood, but if we keep letting them shut us up, they will win. The only way to fight back is to stop being afraid of them. So, I took a stance. This was a good story, and I vowed to stand behind it to the end. If people didn't like it, then they didn't like it. I didn't know what else I could do.

Luckily, the fearless and awesome Dean Cain came on board to play the real-life detective who cracked the case, and the other lead went to a talented actress named Sarah Jane Morris. Sarah Jane played the lead prosecutor of Gosnell (who was also, in real life, a mother of five) —and for her to take that role in a movie that could be seen as "anti-abortion" in Hollywood took a lot of courage. Sarah Jane, a mother herself, was not necessarily conservative, but she saw the story the way I did—that what Gosnell did was horrific, and people should know about it. She played that role with a truly heartbreaking sense of discovery as the mounting horror was revealed to her—a very powerful and touching performance. I'll always be grateful to her for taking it on.

After James Woods passed on the role of Mike Cohan, Gosnell's defense attorney, I ended up doing it myself. While we were writing the script, I knew I could play the part. A lot of what my character says is actual transcribed dialogue from the trial. And the more we read those parts out loud, the more I thought I could definitely play this part. I mean, let's face it. I've played an awful lot of bad guys. This was natural for me.

Of course, there was a big discussion about who we were going to get to play Gosnell. I suggested, perhaps a bit tongue-in-cheek, that we should get Bill Cosby. Everyone thought I was crazy. But, hey, think of the box office now!

The terrific casting directors we hired, Sunday "Sunny" Boling and Meg Morman, had brought up the name Earl Billings as a potential to play Gosnell, and I knew Earl. I'd done an episode of *Seven Days* with him in 1998, and in 2004, he came on and did an episode of *Rodney*. Earl is a great journeyman actor, so I said, "He'll be great. See if he'll do it." Lucky for us, he immediately said yes.

When Earl first came to the set, he laughed and said to me, "I don't know if it's a compliment or not that when Nick Searcy was directing a movie about maybe the most prolific serial killer in American history, he thought, 'Let's call Earl.'"

Earl Billings was absolutely fantastic in the movie. He did his research and came in really well prepared. The producers had actually visited Gosnell in prison, so they had firsthand knowledge of how Kermit Gosnell comes off—as a sweet, caring doctor who thinks he's the nicest, most charming thing in the world. It made the role even creepier, and Earl nailed it. It is the standout performance in the film.

We had success casting local actresses in many of the key supporting roles, even though for many of them, it was their first film. I think that by the time we wrapped, I had five different thank-you notes that all read, "Thank you for giving me my first role."

But there was one role we had a tough time casting: a woman who stops in the middle of her abortion, after she hears the baby's heartbeat, and tells Gosnell that she's not going to go through with it. He tries to stop her from leaving, but she goes to a different hospital and delivers her baby.

It's a very important character—only two scenes, but they're vital to the story. We auditioned a lot of actresses, but I just couldn't find anybody I liked for the role.

We were filming the movie in Oklahoma, and one Sunday, I went to a Waffle House (my favorite restaurant chain by the way) in Oklahoma City. The place was very busy, and the manager was going around apologizing to everybody for their meals being late. I kept looking at her. There was something about her. She was very attractive, and she had a tattoo on her neck. There was a certain toughness about her, and she way she carried herself was so poised and competent. There was a strength and a wisdom to her that I thought would really read on camera.

I felt moved to go and talk to her. I waited until she had a free moment, and I said, "Look, I know this sounds like a crazy pickup line, but...um, have you ever acted in a film before?"

Obviously having never been asked that question, she predictably responded, "Um, no."

I said, "Look, I know this might sound like a cliche pick-up line, but...I really am a director from Hollywood and I'm shooting a movie here in town and there's a part in it that you would be right for. Would you mind if I got the script and let you read it with me to see if it's something you want to do?"

"Um, okay."

I drove home and got the script and went back to the Waffle House and sat down with her in a booth to read the script together. I explained that the character only had three or four lines, but they were very important to the story. I said, "I think you could do this. Would you be willing?"

She was understandably skeptical of this guy who suddenly showed up at her job claiming to be a Hollywood director and offering her a role in a movie. "I don't know. How much would it pay?" she asked.

I said, "Well, it'll probably be at least two or three days of work—and it'll pay about eight hundred and thirty dollars a day."

She said, "Okay, I'll do it."

The first day she came to work, she practically brought her entire family with her to make sure I wasn't some sort of crazy serial killer. We shot with her a couple of days, and she did very well. She was a natural. I kept telling her, "Tessya, don't try to be interesting. You're interesting enough. Just tell the truth. Let the words do the work for you." And she was terrific.

On the third day, one of the producers, Ann, came over to me and said, "You're not going to believe this."

I replied, "Oh no. What now?" I was sure someone had quit, or some location had fallen out, or some other low-budget-movie disaster had occurred.

She said, "The thing that happened to her character in the movie happened to her in real life."

I said, "What are you talking about?"

"Tessya, in her real life, went to have an abortion, and when they let her listen to the heartbeat of the baby, she decided not to go through with the abortion. She had her baby, just like her character in the movie."

I was floored. I felt the hand of God was at play here. I believe God led me to that Waffle House to find her. That something inside me, telling me, when I first saw her, "She can do it! She can do it!"—was Him.

That woman's name is Tessya Whatley, and she has since done some speaking at pro-life conventions telling her incredible story. She is now the proud mother of three boys, including her firstborn, whose heartbeat changed her life.

After filming was completed, I didn't have any control over what the producers did with the film when my directing job was done. At first, they asked me to edit the movie in three weeks, which I told them was insane and impossible. I asked for ten weeks, and we wound up agreeing on seven, which is not enough time for a feature film. That span also included Thanksgiving and Christmas, and I wasn't even given additional time to account for those holidays! On top of that, I'd had knee replacement surgery right after we finished filming. While we were editing, I hobbled down a long outdoor staircase to a basement editing room and sat there with my leg elevated for the whole seven-week period.

During filming, there were some real concerns regarding the budget, concerns that were becoming obvious as we edited the film. For example: we had three and a half days to shoot all of the courtroom scenes, which probably comprised 30 percent of the movie. So, three and a half days was a very short amount of time to shoot all the necessary scenes. My director of photography, Mark Petersen from *Carolina Low* (I can't make a movie without him!) and I had asked for this floating-helium-balloon lighting system. With that system, instead of doing a reset of every light, you can just float it to the other side of the room, and *voila!* you're ready to go with just a few adjustments.

But I was told we didn't have enough money. I kept thinking, *It can't be that much, plus it's going to save us so much time.* In the end, since we didn't have the floating system, we shot all of the scenes in one direction on one day, and on the next day lit the other side of the room and shot all of the scenes in the opposite direction. It was very, very difficult and very tedious. It's hard enough to shoot out of sequence, but when you're shooting the same scene on different days from different angles, it's much harder to keep any continuity.

I was very disappointed in that regard. I also wanted drone shots, which we also never got. There were a lot of things I asked for that would have greatly enhanced the quality of the movie but never received on set. So it's fair to say there was a healthy dose of tension at times between me and the producers.

In retrospect, I know that they were trying to make the best movie they could with the resources they had. And I was trying to do the same. I'm not saying that they're necessarily the bad guys. I might have been the bad guy. I might have been asking for too much. I don't know. Having produced a couple of films after *Gosnell*, I empathize now a bit more than I did then. But the tension definitely continued through the editing process. We weren't really speaking by the end, just leaving each other nasty notes. It was very nerve-wracking trying to finish that film.

However, whatever tensions we had in terms of filming and editing were soon forgotten when the time came to publicize the release. It was all hands on deck. I knew the traditional Hollywood channels, especially film festivals, which are generally run by leftists, would never give this film a chance.

The producers told me what they were planning to do was a theatrical release and then try to sell the film to a streaming service, which I thought was a pretty good strategy. If we could get a really good theatrical release and do well at the box office, then it should be relatively easy to get the movie on some kind of streaming service.

We did a lot of media promotion for the film, including screenings all over the country. They sent me here, and they sent me there. I did the Huckabee show and a screening in Washington, DC. We split up PR duties because I was working on a TV series called *The Hot Zone* at the same time the film was being released.

I think the first-week box office returns were really good. We were number ten overall and the highest-rated independent film of that week. But after that first week, theaters started pulling the movie, even though we were putting up good numbers.

They just didn't want people to see it. I mean, they *really* didn't want people to see it. *Gosnell* got only eleven reviews. Most independent films get between one hundred fifty and two hundred reviews. They did to *Gosnell* what they try to do with all conservative-leaning films that are effective. They don't slam a conservative film. They don't say it's is a terrible movie that you shouldn't go see. They don't say *anything*. They pretend it's not there. They pretend it doesn't exist. And that's how they keep people from seeing the film.

We spent about four to five weeks in the box office. After that, our theatrical run was done.

But *Gosnell* was a story that needed to be told. So many times, I've seen the pro-life and pro-choice proponents talk past each other. And a lot of times, we don't know exactly what it is we're talking about.

There's a scene in the movie where I'm interrogating the "good" abortion doctor, played by Janine Turner, who does everything the right way. I have her take us step-by-step through what they do in a legal abortion. This is the scene that, when I first read it, made me want to direct the film.

I found the exchange between the defense attorney and the doctor shocking—because I had no idea what an abortion actually was, what the steps were, how it was done. I didn't know that they stick a needle into the baby's heart while it's still in the womb and inject it with a poison that stops the heart, and then extract it with forceps—sometimes piece by piece. I didn't know that. And I think that everyone *should* know that.

I wasn't attempting, with *Gosnell*, to make everyone agree with the pro-life position. I wanted to make a movie that put us all on the same page, information-wise. Let's all know exactly what it is we're talking about before we form our opinion about it.

Today, *Gosnell* is available to buy or rent on a number of streaming services, and I encourage everyone reading this to do so. It holds up pretty well.

CHAPTER 12

AMERICA, AMERICA, GOD SHED HIS GRACE ON THEE

In the winter of 2020, right at the beginning of the COVID lockdown nonsense, a man named Jeff Hunt, one of the executive directors of the Western Conservative Summit (which meets every year in Colorado), called me with an interesting proposition. Jeff had seen a speech I had recently given at a meeting of the Council for National Policy, about how conservatives needed to start making films. Jeff said that the WCS was not going to able to meet in person that year, due to all the virus hysteria, and they had voted to make a documentary film instead, which they would premiere as part of their online summit—and he wanted to know if I'd be willing to do it.

Their idea was to make a documentary about the relationship between the Bible and the Constitution, by interviewing politicians and thought leaders across America, and call it *America, America, God Shed His Grace on Thee.*

I hesitated. "You know, Jeff, I've never made a documentary. I don't know if I'd be right for what you're looking for."

But the more I thought about it, I began to see what a unique opportunity this was for me. I had been going around giving speeches, like the one that opens this book that I gave at Hillsdale College, about how conservatives needed to get into the film business—and here was someone giving me an opportunity to put his money where my mouth was. I'd been praying for an opportunity to make my own films, instead of just being an actor for hire, and here was another chance. I called my friend Chris Burgard, with whom I'd worked before on the hilarious *Acting School with Nick Searcy* web series (which is still up on YouTube) and who had also made a documentary called *Border* a few years back.

After getting Chris on board, I called Jeff back and said, "I'm in!" The next day, they gave us the contract. The film was designed to be a series of interviews with leading figures of the religious and conservative movements, and they had a long list of people they wanted me to contact.

I put together a schedule for a five-week shoot, because it was already April, and they wanted a finished film by October 10, only six months away. During those five weeks, we traveled all around the country, setting up thirty-five to forty interviews from coast to coast. And what great interviews. We interviewed influencers like: Alveda King, Ben Shapiro, Michael Knowles, Richard Grenell, and our old friend Herman Cain. Chris and I, during Herman's 2012 campaign for president, made a comedic short film called *He Carried Yellow Flowers* endorsing him, which Herman, because of his great sense of humor, found hilarious, and we had been friends ever since. *Flowers* was also the inspiration for my

Acting School series, in which I play an insufferable, egotistical movie star named Nick Searcy. It was quite a stretch.

We were filming right in the middle of COVID, and *no one* was going to the airports. It was bizarre to have an entire airplane to ourselves. We put together a crew of six people, including my son, Omar, and my faithful friend Mark Petersen from *Carolina Low* and *Gosnell*.

After a few interviews in Los Angeles, we flew to Atlanta, where we interviewed Alveda King, Mr. Cain, and Ambassador Andrew Young, and filmed in front of Martin Luther King's Ebenezer Baptist Church. After my experience with the touring production of *I Have a Dream* years before, this was a very powerful moment for me. We then drove up through my hometown, Cullowhee, North Carolina, and filmed a little vignette at my home church, Cullowhee Baptist, spending the night with my parents to save the production a little money. Then it was on to Washington, DC for a week of scheduled shoots. We filmed interviews in front of the steps of the Lincoln Memorial, inside the Jefferson Memorial, in front of the Capitol, and everything was deserted. Congressman Louie Gohmert took us inside the Capitol Building, and the silence was deafening. It was a ghost town—like it was a movie set that we purchased.

I also discovered the miracle of the electric scooters, which were on every corner, it seemed, that you could rent using your iPhone. I found it one day trying to get to the Jefferson Memorial in time for our interview with James Golden, or "Bo Snerdley" as Rush fans would know him. I was going to be late because I had a long walk from where we had to park, and I came across this scooter, figured out how to turn it on with my credit card, and off I went. The scooter subsequently became a recurring theme in the movie. My character, The Man in the Suit, who did all the interviews and wore the same costume throughout the film, would go from interview to interview on a scooter. It gave us some great comic relief and kept the movie flowing.

But on our third day in DC, we got a call from Herman Cain, three days after we had interviewed him, from a hospital in Atlanta, saying he had tested positive for COVID. And of course, at that time, everybody was in a panic; everybody thought COVID meant a probable death sentence. So the crew voted to shut everything down and go home for a week. And that's what we did. (Sadly, our friend Herman Cain never made it out of the hospital, and our interview with him became the last he would ever give. Herman had been battling many other medical issues, which we were unaware of at the time. The Left loves to say that Herman "died of COVID." He didn't—just like most of the other people the Left claims "died of COVID." But that's another story.)

Even at home, we were all on pins and needles. My son, Omar, was working on the show with me. My daughter and my wife rigged up a system of plastic frames that covered the doors and hallways, dividing the house in half so Omar and I could only be on one side and they could only be on the other. It's funny to look back on it now, but it shows how ridiculously we were all acting at the time—because of the lies about COVID that we were being told by Fauci and others.

I was always very skeptical about that whole coronavirus thing. I never believed it from the beginning. A couple of the crew did test positive, but they got over the virus in a few days, and thankfully nobody got too sick. A few days later, we were right back on the road.

One of the very best interviews we conducted was with Andrew Young, who had marched with Martin Luther King Jr. and served as US ambassador to the United Nations under Jimmy Carter. Andrew Young was a Democrat, and a friend of the project recommended that we try to reach out to him, which we did. And even though it was a conservative project, Andrew Young said, "Anybody that wants to talk about God and America can come talk to me." His interview is just riveting. It is the most unexpected and moving interview in the film.

Our movie makes the point that Martin Luther King Jr. was not only a political activist, he was, first and foremost, a minister, and everything that he did was based on the Bible and his relationship with God. Young, who marched with Dr. King and was an integral part of the civil rights movement, told us a story about visiting Martin Luther King Jr. in jail.

The desk sergeant at the Birmingham jail was horrible to Young—called him the N-word and was disrespectful and dismissive. Young quoted the sergeant as saying to his superior, "Hey, there's a little (N-word) out here that wants to go see the big (N-word) in the back. What do I do?"

But even in the face of the desk sergeant's hardened racism, Young was respectful to him. Young saw that the desk sergeant was a large man and asked him where he had played football, and by the end of Dr. King's term in jail, the sergeant was treating him almost like a friend, smiling and waving him in whenever he came to visit Dr. King.

Andrew Young told us that about thirty years later, in New England during a book signing, a man came up to him and said, "I'll bet you don't remember me. I was the desk sergeant in Birmingham, Alabama, when you visited with Dr. King."

"My goodness, you've lost a lot of weight!" Young said.

And the man said to Andrew Young, "I've lost a lot of things. You changed my life forever. The way you treated me with kindness, the way you stopped and talked to me, made me see that the racism that I had in my heart was wrong. And I resigned from that police department very shortly after that and moved my family up north. And I've changed, because of you."

That interview gets me every time I see it.

The movie was released for free on October 10, 2020, and it was very well received. The WCS directors were expecting to get thirty thousand views or so, and they got three hundred thousand, and it was just a hit for them. But in retrospect, the film was a little too funny in places and a little too risqué in places for the people who sponsored the movie. They actually objected to Andrew Young's story because he says the N-word out loud in the film.

It shouldn't have been an issue, but we went back and forth with them about that. We argued that Young was telling a story about his own experience, he's black himself, and he was using the language that he heard. Bleeping the word out would harm the impact of the desk sergeant's transformation. That story is the embodiment of one of MLK's most memorable quotes, one that I think of often: "We must meet hate with love."

We won that fight, but ultimately, I don't think the powers that be at the Western Conservative Summit were all that happy with the tone of *God Shed*. At the end of the day, we were making a film for people who aren't filmmakers, but educators and academics, politicians and philosophers, so they didn't put as much stock in the film's entertainment value. They were looking for it to be more like a term paper, an academic presentation, factual and filled with content.

They were always pushing for me to add more interviews and to cut out some of the humor, but in my opinion, the film worked better *because* of the humor. If we didn't break it up with humor, people would get bored and tune out. I got a lot of comments about how the humor was so unexpected that when it came up, it kept people engaged.

The agreement in the contract was that I could edit the film the way I wanted, but they had the right to tell me to take out something if they objected to it. For example, there was a small section in the film about the controversial moment when Trump, after the Black Lives Matter rioters had tried to burn the famous St. John's cathedral down, had walked across the White House lawn, stood in front of the church in Washington and simply held up a Bible. The Democrats roared that he was exploiting the situation. Former Ambassador Richard Grenell was with Trump right before he walked to the church. Grenell told us why he did it, and it was in the middle of a rather lengthy section about why the Democrats hated Trump so much.

Grenell said that Trump went because he wanted to send this message: you can peacefully protest all you want, you're allowed to disagree with the government, but you cannot burn down a church that has been an integral part of America's history for two hundred years.

I saw it as Trump, perhaps in a less than eloquent way, standing up for religious liberty in America by showing that we're not going to allow protests like these to undercut the religious basis on which this nation was founded—which is EXACTLY what the Left wants to do.

The left-wing media's criticism of Trump was all, "He's exploiting this tragedy," or "He's trying to draw attention to himself," or "He's such a hypocrite; he's not a religious man, why is behaving this way?" that sort of thing. It was never confusing to me. So I thought it'd be a good idea to get that out and explain it, to get what I thought was Trump's side of the story out to the public, because he'd been so vilified by the monolithic media.

But the Western Conservative Summit asked us to take a part of that section of the film out. They were a 501(c)(3) nonprofit organization and feared that if they were seen as overtly political, it could cause some issues for them. They were afraid that section might be taken as an endorsement of Trump. We, unfortunately, ended up leaving some of it on the cutting-room floor.

We interviewed the president of Colorado Christian University in the film, and when I asked him about Trump, he literally put his head down on his desk and said, "Do we have to talk about him?" Of course, I put that in the first cut of the film because I thought it was hilarious—and also showed how controversial President Trump was among Republicans as well as leftist Democrats. But we were asked to cut that out too.

A great song from John Rich, "Earth to God," closes the film. John is a good friend whom I met when we were both guests on Greg Gutfeld's show. His song made the end of the film soar.

For a seventy-minute film, we covered a lot of ground. Brilliantly edited by my friend John Quinn, editor of *Gosnell*, the film covers communism, bias in the media, and even bias in the entertainment world. We used the 1960 film *Inherit the Wind* as a prime example. It's based on a Broadway play that purports to tell the story of the Scopes trial, but, as usual, the film is full of lies. The film made the Christian apologist, played by Frederic March, look like an old fool and the Darwinian lawyer (Spencer Tracy) look like a smart, tolerant, rational person, but that's not how the trial actually transpired. In real life, the religious side actually won the case, but of course Hollywood made the religious side look like stupid, fanatical losers.

We also have the great writer David Horowitz, famous son of full-on Communist radicals who saw the light and became a conservative, discussing the Supreme Court decision on getting prayer out of schools and about how systematically the government has drummed God out of the public square. His hilarious takedown of atheist Madalyn Murray O'Hair, who won the case that removed God from schools, is not to be missed.

We premiered the film before a live audience at Godspeak Calvary Chapel in Newbury Park, California. Because it was one of the few churches in California that was open during the pandemic, we had interviewed the minister Rob McCoy and filmed the church service on the very Sunday that the

State of California had threatened to shut down his church and arrest the people who attended that day. It is perhaps the most active and powerful section of the film, showing in real life how the Left used the pandemic to stifle religion by declaring the church "non-essential" while keeping strip clubs, liquor stores, and marijuana dispensaries open. Rob has since become a friend and mentor to me, and I now consider him to be my pastor. The response from the audience was fantastic: weeping and joyful at the end. It was a wonderful treat to able to watch the film with a live audience—if only to hear them laugh at my jokes!

I didn't get much feedback from my friends on the Hollywood Left. I think, as they do with most conservative-leaning films, they just pretended it didn't exist. The conservative side of my Hollywood friends who share my politics, they loved the film. They watched it over and over again and bought copies for their friends. But, just like *Gosnell*, I really didn't set out to make a partisan film.

However, I did make a few jokes about Democrats. There's a section at the beginning where I'm calling people in Congress to try to get them to do an interview and talk about God and America. I call famous anti-Semitic Congresswoman Ilhan Omar's office and ask to speak to her, saying, "I'm making a film about God in America…" There's a long pause, and then I say, "Well, is her husband there? Or her brother, or whatever?"

One of my Democratic friends who did see the film objected, "You know, you shouldn't have made fun of her. She's taking a lot of flak for that."

To which I replied, "She is a proven anti-Semite who hates this country and is utterly ungrateful for the life she is able to have here that she could not have had where she came from. And also—allegedly marrying her brother is kind of weird, right? I think she deserves a little pushback on that!"

And that's the whole divide, to me. They can make all the stupid jokes about Republicans and conservatives they want, but if you make a joke about one of theirs, you're a bully. We've put up with Democrats our whole lives in Hollywood. We've tolerated them, worked with them, heard them spew their nonsense, and most of us conservative actors still follow the unwritten rule that it is impolite to talk politics or religion at work. We are there to make a product that is very difficult to make, and you don't want to do anything that can slow that process by pissing everyone off. But the Hollywood Left functions like they're the only people in the room and there's no possibility anybody in the room could disagree with them—and if anybody does, the leftists want to make sure they know that they're not welcome there.

That's why Hollywood is so divided, and that's why the product coming out of Hollywood is so monolithically leftist. The Left cannot bear to allow the other side to speak. That's why we're labeled "Nazis" or "racists" or "white supremacists." They have to demonize us and call us names rather than answering our arguments—which they can't do.

Making *God Shed* toughened me up. The partisan reaction to it added to the freedom I felt after *Gosnell*—that I was doing the right thing and didn't care what the Left thought of me anymore. I felt like I was doing what one of my heroes, Andrew Breitbart, had told us we must do: engage in culture, because politics is downstream of culture. This led me to make my most controversial film to date, set me on a path that I could not have seen coming—and helped me enter the most satisfying portion of my career: the making of *Capitol Punishment.*

CHAPTER 13

CAPITOL PUNISHMENT THE MOVIE (OR HOW I BECAME A WHITE SUPREMACIST RACIST INSURRECTIONIST TERRORIST)

On January 1, 2021, I had no intention of going to Washington, DC on January 6. I'd planned a trip back to North Carolina on January 7, but Chris Burgard called and said he was going to DC, that it was going to be an important day in history, and that he thought we should be there to see it. After a bit of deliberation, I decided to change my flight plans, and go to Washington on the fifth, attend Trump's speech, and then travel on to NC on the seventh.

There was no thought in my head at that time of making a film. I went to witness the day and to stand with the American people who, like me, believed that the election was stolen. (I still believe this, by the way. I know the Democrats want to make it illegal to believe the election stolen, but they haven't succeeded yet.) So, as I continually tell Chris, my presence in Washington that day was *all* his fault. He talked me into it.

I wound up oversleeping the morning of January 6, so I didn't get to the Ellipse in time to get close to the President's speech. I spent most of the day just observing and talking to the people who were there, and who seemed to be a very patriotic, happy crowd—and absolutely the largest crowd I'd ever seen. There were people of all races and religions, all sharing their support for President Trump. As far as I could tell, it was a joyful gathering of people singing "The Star-Spangled Banner," reciting the Pledge of Allegiance, and praying for America. It was a great display of patriotism.

After Trump's speech was over, I walked toward the Capitol with a lot of other people, and I wound up on the east side of the Capitol Building, between it and the Supreme Court Building, standing with thousands of others behind the bike racks the police had set up as barriers—although, suspiciously, that was a pretty insubstantial barrier, in hindsight.

I'd told my friend Bo Snerdley (James Golden, Rush's longtime friend and call screener) that I would be there that day, and he set it up for me to call in to *The Rush Limbaugh Show*. Todd Herman, who was filling in for Rush that day, asked me to characterize the crowd, and I said, among other things, "It's basically a very patriotic, happy, well-informed crowd. They're talking about the process they want to see happen, and that they would like for the Senate to challenge the results so that the certification could be postponed for ten days so they can audit and make sure that the election results were correct."

(Ironically, when I listen to the playback of Rush's show that day, what was on right before I called in was audio of what was going on inside the Capitol. Congressman Paul

Gosar of Arizona had just risen to challenge the counting of his state's electoral votes—and at the time, Mike Pence accepted that challenge, saying that since it was "an objection submitted in writing and signed by both a representative and a senator, it complies with the law, Chapter One of Title Three of the United States Code. The clerk will record the objection."

I say this to people all the time: This was *exactly* what everyone who went to Washington that day *wanted to happen*. So why would they be trying to obstruct the proceeding? Why were so many of these people charged with "disrupting an official proceeding" when the proceeding—pausing the vote and auditing the results—was what they wanted? But I digress...)

While I was behind the barricades, I occasionally saw people in masks and mostly black gear go up to the barricades and rattle them, scream obscenities, and make violent gestures toward the police—not actual violence, just screaming and gesticulating. And every time that happened, the people around me would shout them down, yelling "Stop that! That's not us! That's not MAGA! *We don't do that!*" It didn't really hit me at the time, but looking back, there was definitely an element in the crowd, small but vocal, that did not seem to be on the same page as those that were praying and singing.

At a certain point, I saw the Capitol Police remove the barricades and motion people to come on toward the Capitol—which I thought was very strange. But of course, when the police did that, people thought it was okay to come forward, and so they did, waving flags and singing songs. There was a lady with a little jam box on rollers playing the Twisted Sister tune "We're Not Gonna Take It" on a loop, so everyone started singing that. They came toward the Capitol Building, not in a rush but at a normal pace, and got up on the stairs, waving their flags and singing "We're Not Gonna Take It!"

I never went up the stairs that day; I was at the bottom filming with my iPhone, and I never saw anybody enter the building. I did hear some sharp noises that sounded like flash-bangs, but they were on the other side of the building. I took an awful lot of short videos and pictures of that day, and when I look at them, I see droves of happy, laughing, joyful people—that's what I remember from that day. I never felt a bit of danger on that side of the building. Soon after that, my phone died. I remember it was very cold, and I thought to myself that the event was pretty much over and I'd walk back to the Airbnb we'd rented that was fairly close to the Capitol. A large part of the crowd left at the same time. On my walk back, they had closed all the roads and wouldn't even let anybody walk down the streets. There were armed National Guardsmen surrounding the entire area, which also was strange.

I sat down on at a sidewalk table in front of a restaurant that happened to be across from the garage where members of Congress park. I began to see them leaving in their cars, one by one, and the guards were protecting their departure. At this point, I still didn't know what had happened. I later learned that there supposedly had been bomb threats against the Democratic National Committee and the Republican National Committee. News reports claimed that officials had found a pipe bomb, or something that looked like one, in front of the DNC headquarters. (Funny how, to this day, they have not found the supposed bomber. They can track down every sixty-five-year-old grandmother that walked into the Capitol for thirty seconds in the middle of a huge crowd being waved in by police, but they can't find the lone bomber that they have on surveillance camera footage? I don't buy that for a second.)

Chris and I had gotten separated for the entire day. He was filming on one side of the Capitol, and I was shooting with my iPhone on the other—again, not with the idea of making a film, but filming like a tourist. When we finally met back at our Airbnb, we started to put together notes about what we'd seen. When we turned on the news that night, we saw the whole break-in at the Capitol and all this violence that neither of us had seen.

The news didn't show the size of the crowd. All they focused on were the people around and inside the Capitol—and how did they know to have their cameras only there, by the way? Most of the people who went inside that afternoon were sightseers. A lot of them were people whom the police had told it was okay to come in, and as videos showed, most of them were staying within the little roped-off walkway areas and weren't committing any acts of vandalism or violence.

But all you saw on the news was the supposed "insurrection" and all the terrible things the media wanted us so desperately to believe that President Trump had stirred up in an attempted coup. The next morning, I flew out of Washington, DC, very confused and disturbed by the disparity between what I had personally witnessed and what was being shown on every cable and network outlet. It didn't make any sense.

When I went back to North Carolina on January 7, the plan was to visit my family and spend about a month there with my parents. At the time, my mom and dad were thinking about vacating their property, and my wife and I were considering taking it over.

That first Saturday night after I got home, I was in bed when I got a call from my theatrical agent. This shocked me, because my agent almost never called me—we communicated primarily through email at the time—and never on a weekend after business hours. I answered with a surprised, "Hey, Dan, what's up?"

"I just have to ask you one question. Did you go into the building?"

"What building? What are you talking about?"

"You went to Washington on January sixth, right? Did you enter the Capitol Building?" Dan asked.

"No, I didn't go into any buildings. I didn't even see anybody go into the Capitol. I had no idea anyone went into the building until I saw the news. Why?"

"Well, there's a casting director out here passing a picture around to all the agents and casting directors of someone there that day that she claims is you, and she is telling them you should never work again." Dan was quite breathless and excited. I got the feeling that Dan had called me fully prepared to drop me as a client.

"Send me the picture," I said.

It was a picture of a man wearing a cap and with a mask covering his face, waving a flag, standing on the Capitol steps in front of a mural. Even though his head and face were covered, it was obvious that it wasn't me.

"Dan, come on," I said. "That guy outweighs me by about fifty pounds. You know that isn't me."

"Well, I didn't think so, but I had to make sure."

"Well, who is spreading this rumor?"

Shockingly, the casting director was someone I had known for thirty years, since my days starting out in New York City. She had cast me in some of the most important projects in my career. I had once done, as a friend, a public reading of her husband's play. We were friends, or so I thought. It was hard to believe.

Since I had her personal email address (and she had mine as well; she could have just asked me herself), I dropped her a line, saying in part:

> We've known each other a long time. I remember doing a reading of your husband's play about how awful Republicans are. I believe that people have the right to express themselves, and tell the stories they want to tell. As a professional actor, I am willing to participate in that, even if sometimes I don't agree with the POV.
>
> You write my reps and tell them that you're "disturbed" by my perspective? Sounds like an attempt at intimidation to me.
>
> You could have reached out to me for verification. Why didn't you? That is disturbing to me...
>
> I find it very sad, after knowing you for 30 years or so, that you would treat me this way. But having worked in Hollywood for the same amount

of time, I can't say that it surprises me. See you around, Nick

She responded with:

I reached out to your reps after another casting director sent me a photo of you on the Capitol steps waving a flag with a big mural behind you and it turns out it wasn't you. I only did it out of concern for you and for your career. We have known each other for forever and I want you to know that I would never prevent you from getting work. I can separate politics from acting. I'm still a fan. And when it comes to politics we can agree to disagree.

I have never heard from this person again, nor have I since been offered a role by the major network for which she is head of casting. And she's not the only one. There are at least three casting directors whom I had worked for so many times over the years that I knew their families, their children's names, and they knew my family as well. After January 6, I've never heard from any of them again. When someone asks me if Hollywood has a "blacklist," I tell them this story. There may not necessarily be a physical list, but Hollywood leftists keep score.

As the "insurrection!" narrative began being pushed by the media, about how everybody who went to Washington that day was a white supremacist racist insurrectionist terrorist piece of garbage, it made people afraid to speak up and say it wasn't true. Which, of course, is what it was designed to do.

This is a campaign of fear and intimidation by the government, and it has been from the beginning.

The leftists in the government and the media began coming after people who just were standing in the crowd. The federal government put up billboards all over America, saying in effect, "If you know anybody who went to Washington on January 6, they must be reported to the FBI, and here's the number." They turned neighbors, and in some cases family members, into informants for the American version of the Gestapo. It disgusted me, and it continues to this day. The weaponization of the federal law enforcement and judicial systems against American citizens is not in any way slowing down. It is ramping up, with over 1,100 people already arrested, and the government pledging to arrest at least a thousand more—even now, nearly three years after the day.

About a month later, Chris Burgard and I were in Florida screening our documentary *God Shed His Grace on Thee* at a meeting of the Council for National Policy. At the Q&A after the screening, one of the people in attendance asked, "If you could make another documentary, what would you make it about?"

Chris said, "We'd do it about January sixth and tell the truth about what really transpired that day."

A man walked up to us as soon as the film ended and asked, "How much would you need to make that movie?" And so it began.

We started interviewing people who were in Washington on January 6 and subsequently had been arrested or raided in the early morning hours by an overkill of dozens of SWAT members and armored vehicles. I said from the beginning that our biggest responsibility was to humanize these Americans that the Democrats and the Democrat-controlled media had demonized. More and more we found that these were normal, working-class people—church goers, veterans, police officers, people who had never been arrested before— who were suddenly being treated like the most dangerous violent criminals, drug dealers, cartel leaders, or serial killers. The FBI came with SWAT teams and armored vehicles to their houses in predawn raids—a massive show of force designed to humiliate them in front of their neighbors than for any real reason or precaution. The FBI stormed in as if they thought these people were going to blow up buildings and start killing people.

These actions were so over the top as to be insane. That's why the movie became known as *Capitol Punishment*, because the more we looked at the situation, it became clear that the federal government was trying to punish anyone who went to Washington on January 6 to exercise their First Amendment rights and protest an election they believed was illegitimate— and to instill fear in anyone who might consider protesting any future election. The government's actions were clearly meant to intimidate and terrorize, not to protect.

Capitol Punishment was released on Thanksgiving Day 2021, and it was the first documentary to show the excesses of law enforcement and the way that the federal government and its agencies, including the Department of Justice and the FBI, conspired to suppress dissent and to crush people who dared to speak out against them. And they haven't stopped. In fact, many of the people who appeared in my film have been sentenced to prison.

Easton Cantwell, an Army veteran and business owner from my hometown of Sylva, North Carolina, pled guilty, after months of harassment and being bankrupted by the process of defending himself, and was sentenced to five months in prison. He had to report to prison in January 2023. He was on the Capitol stairs, but all he did was help a lady who was being pinned by a door who was caught in the crush of the crowd. Easton yelled "Hold the door!" and pulled her out, and then yelled something like, "We need more patriots up here." For those words, he was charged with inciting a riot.

That's the type of "crime" we've discovered in most of the cases related to January 6. And the intimidation doesn't stop with the government sending the FBI after these people—the corrupt Department of Justice loads them up with multiple charges. They tell them they're facing thirty-eight years in prison and will go in front of a District of Columbia jury (which will be 99 percent Democrat, just like most of the court-appointed public defenders), and they can't even bring in a lawyer from out of state.

To argue a case in the District of Columbia, you have to be licensed to practice law in the District of Columbia, and as a result, most of these people end up with a defense attorney who basically despises them, thinks they're guilty, and wants them to go to jail. The jury despises them and wants them to go to jail too, and then they're sentenced by a judge who hates them and calls them "insurrectionists" (even though no one has yet been charged with insurrection). So a lot of people end up taking a plea deal, because they believe they have no chance of being exonerated.

Sarah McAbee, the wife of Ronald Colton McAbee, a Tennessee deputy sheriff who was convicted in October 2023 of five felonies after being held without bail for over two years, told me a very chilling story. She was preparing to hire a very good—and expensive—defense attorney, having raised a considerable amount of money for her husband's defense. When the attorney found out Colton wasn't going to take a plea deal and cop to something that he didn't do, he advised her to just take a public defender and save her money for the appeal. Any January 6 defendants tried in a DC court are going to be convicted, no matter how good their defense is. The jury has them convicted in their minds before the trial starts, and in most cases, they barely deliberate at all. Colton was convicted on all counts, even though it was shown at his trial that he did not attack a police officer, that the police officer actually thanked him for his help, and that he tried to save Roseanne Boyland's life. It is shameful.

This is precisely why no judge has granted a change-of-venue motion in any of the January 6 cases. They want these people tried in DC because they know if they allowed them to be tried in their home states of Florida or Texas or Oklahoma or North Carolina, by a jury of their *actual* peers and not the hateful 99 percent Democrat jury pool of Washington, DC, that most of these people would be exonerated. And if they were to be exonerated, it would expose the utter lie of the entire "insurrection" narrative—and they cannot allow that to happen.

To date, the defendants that have refused pleas deals and gone to trial face a 99.4 percent conviction rate. So I cannot blame those who look at this untenable situation and decide to plead guilty to one charge just to get their trial behind them and serve less time. Because they have seen horrible judges like Tim Kelly, Colleen Kollar-Kotelly, Amit Mehta, and others, punish those who dare defend themselves at trial with years in prison—as happened to John Strand.

John Strand refused to plead guilty to something he did not do and went through a jury trial. He mounted a strong and credible defense, and at the end of it, the jury deliberated for less than half an hour and found him guilty on all charges. He was sentenced to three years, and he told me that as he left the courtroom, one of the jurors gave him the finger. The level of hatred that has been instilled in the DC jury pool by the Democrats and their media accomplices is truly breathtaking. By comparison, the person he was with that day, Dr. Simone Gold, who had been invited to give a speech and whom Strand was there to protect, did every single thing that John did, went everywhere he went, and took a plea deal and served around thirty days.

Another thing I learned while making this movie is that when you accept a plea deal, you have to sign a statement that the government writes for you, and you have to sign it *whether it is true or not*. In other words, the government is threatening you with a lengthy prison sentence if you do not *lie* and say you did something you did not do. It's like something out of Solzhenitsyn's *Gulag Archipelago*, something the secret police would do in Stalin's USSR: *Sign ze papers or you will never see your children again, traitor!*

It is disgusting to see that this is how our government is now operating. There are a couple of families in Lake Elsinore, California, the Kinnison family and the Martinez family. They're regular people, living in a little suburban neighborhood, and at six o'clock one morning in June 2021, armored vehicles rolled up and SWAT teams began banging on their doors and dragging them out of their homes.

Derek Kinnison testified that when he came out of his house, hands up, there were laser dots all over his chest. Tony Martinez's thirteen-year-old daughter was dragged from their house and handcuffed on the sidewalk. None of this was necessary. These are not violent people. These are the kind of people that you would expect the FBI to call and ask questions about what happened on January 6.

The *only* reason for such tactics by the FBI was to spread fear, to terrorize and demonize these people in front of their neighbors. They wanted to scare them to death, and they also wanted their neighbors to believe that these people are dangerous, hateful terrorists—I mean, why else would there have been such a show of force? Such actions are deliberate, and they are evil. But for these people, the punishment didn't stop there. They were ostracized by their neighbors. They lost their jobs, their homes, their friends, their businesses.

Easton Cantwell had three successful coffee shops in western North Carolina. After he was arrested on charges related to January 6, all of the businesses were shut down. News of his arrest was widely published in the newspapers, and everybody who frequented his coffee shops started writing Yelp reviews saying, "I'm not going to go to that white supremacist's coffee shop anymore!"

These people are being deliberately destroyed by the Left. And when the prosecutors make them plead guilty to a felony, that makes them ineligible to vote and to own a firearm legally. They are neutralizing these people. And that is also part of the leftists' strategy—to change the electorate and make it so that people who don't agree with them can't participate in the electoral system.

I never thought I would see the American government act in such a totalitarian fashion. I didn't think it was possible. But it is happening, with the full endorsement of the media and a large swath of our fellow Americans cheering it on. Remember that old saw about "it can't happen here?"

It's happening.

The monolithic media and their brainwashed, slavish audience have a new favorite word: *insurrection*. They use the word when referring to the January 6 events to make it seem like it was a day of violence caused by a bunch of armed white supremacists. But a real insurrection is an attempt to overthrow the government. Throughout history, when people try to stage an insurrection, they bring a few guns, you know? A pistol or two, a butter knife, *something*. But no one who went to the Capitol that day to exercise their right of free speech had a single gun on them. Only the police had guns. And Capitol Police officer Michael Byrd used one to kill an unarmed American veteran, Ashli Babbitt.

You can't have an insurrection just by carrying flags. You have to bring weapons, and the Left is calling January 6 an insurrection because they are trying to make it seem like a violent act committed by terrorists when it wasn't. The other thing the leftist media and politicians leave out (especially the January 6 committee) is that if they really were trying to get to the bottom of what happened, they would not be lying about the fact that there were Antifa and BLM operatives in the crowd dressed as Trump supporters inciting a lot of the violence.

There's no question that there were a few Trump supporters who got caught up in the moment and were angry and did some things they shouldn't have. But a lot of that was instigated by BLM and a team of people we show in our film changing clothes in the bushes—changing out of their black gear into MAGA gear, red hats, and Trump T-shirts. There is also the fact that there were FBI operatives in that crowd, and that the Capitol Police allowed people into the building.

If they were really interested in telling the truth about what happened on January 6, they would reveal these things. FBI Director Christopher Wray got up in front of Congress and said that there was no evidence of BLM/Antifa presence at the Capitol. I have the evidence in my film. It's undeniable that there was indeed a BLM/Antifa presence there. The only people killed that day were Trump supporters.

Ashli Babbitt was shot by officer Michael Byrd. There is video evidence showing Rosanne Boyland was beaten by Capitol Police while she lay on the ground dying. Benjamin Phillips and Kevin Greeson died of heart attacks, Phillips after being hit by a flash-bang grenade. Most of the violence was initiated by either the police or operatives who had infiltrated the crowd, a fact the media and government are covering up. They are doing so because they have a narrative that they have to keep pushing through the 2024 election: that everyone at the Capitol that day was a violent extremist white supremacist insurrectionist domestic terrorist whom evil Donald Trump had sent to Washington to "overthrow democracy."

The word *insurrection* itself is a lie. What happened on January 6 was not an insurrection. It was a protest that turned into a riot—and not even a particularly violent riot. When you look at the BLM riots the year before, and all the buildings that were burned, the people who were murdered, the police cars set on fire, the federal and state buildings set on fire, what happened on January 6 doesn't compare in the slightest.

And yet all you hear from corrupt puppets like Joe Biden and Kamala Harris, as well as their faithful mouthpieces in the media, is that January sixth was the worst thing to happen since the Civil War—worse than 9/11, Pearl Harbor, Hiroshima and World War I all put together. It's utter nonsense. They are liars, and they are trying to demonize anybody who stands up and says the 2020 election was not on the up-and-up. There are a lot of strange things that happened, and they don't want anyone to question their stolen elections ever again.

But it is my prayer that now that the 40,000 hours of video footage that had been withheld—for "national security reasons," don't you know—have finally been released, the whole truth about that day will be revealed, and the political prisoners of January 6, many of whom did absolutely nothing wrong, will be exonerated.

We premiered *Capitol Punishment* at Godspeak Calvary Chapel in Newbury Park, California, on November 7, 2021. The audience was absolutely shocked by what they saw. The rare times we have been able to watch the film with an audience have been very gratifying—and most of the people who see it, say the same thing: "I had no idea this was happening."

But the release of the movie was not as successful as we'd hoped, due to a number of reasons. For example, we were so suppressed on Google that it was hard to find the film with a search. One really had to look long and hard and know the name of the website to find us. The way Western Journal had constructed their website was confusing to a lot of people. We would have around three hundred thousand visitors, but less than 1 percent of them would actually purchase the film because the process was so technically problematic. Also, the website was attacked repeatedly, making it very difficult to get the word out about the film.

But over the course of a year, the investors were paid back, so the venture was successful. However, I do wish the release been handled differently, and we had not been so thoroughly suppressed by the leftists in charge of social media. It's the same thing that happened with *Gosnell*. If there is a film that the leftists don't want people to see, they don't criticize it, or argue with it, or give it a bad review. They don't want to have to argue with the facts presented in *Capitol Punishment*— because they can't. So they pretend like the film doesn't exist.

Unfortunately, that is true of most of the people in this country who identify with the Left and call themselves Democrats. They won't even risk allowing themselves to see another side of the story. For example, my agent at the time, who had represented me for over six years, refused to watch *Capitol Punishment*, because he was afraid it might shake up his narrative and ruin his feeling of superiority over those insurrectionist animals that tried to overthrow democracy. (And this was after I explained to him that America was a republic, not a democracy, because a direct democracy is mob rule—three wolves voting to eat two sheep—but I guess they don't teach civics in Hollywood.) So I fired him. I have a manager still, but I have been just fine without an agent ever since. Why be represented by someone who will not even watch the work you do?

I have friends and even family members who refuse to watch *CP* because it might shake up their view of themselves, and they might have to admit they were wrong, or that conservatives aren't monsters. The media has made them so comfortable with their sneering, condescending hatred of conservatives, has made them feel so justified (pardon the pun) in judging their fellow Americans, that they cannot imagine life without that hatred.

But even more shocking and disappointing has been the lack of support coming from the so-called "conservative" network, Fox News. While OANN ran Capitol Punishment on their network as alternative programming to Liz Cheney's execrable January 6 TV special, Fox News would not even allow us to buy ads for Capitol Punishment on their network. Furthermore, I had been a frequent guest on the network, appearing many times on Red Eye and the Greg Gutfeld Show, and going all the way back to appearances on the O-Reilly Factor. Since Jan. 6, 2021, I have not appeared on Fox News. Many conservative radio hosts and podcasters, including Tim Pool, Dinesh D-Souza, Eric Metaxas, Jason Whitlock, and others, did have me on to talk about it—but quite a few rather famous outlets did not, some even outright admitting that they were afraid to take a stand on the plight of the J6ers.

Regardless, the work continues. I am currently in the process of editing the sequel, *Capitol Punishment 2: The War on Truth*. I want to leave a record of what the lies of the Left have done to this country, the pain they have caused and the lives they have ruined—all over politics, all to destroy Donald Trump and anyone who votes for him, all to cover up the corrupt system they have created, and the crimes they have committed. The blatant and obvious corruption of Biden and his entire family is one of the many reasons they can never give up the narrative of January 6. In fact, the reason the decrepit, incontinent, and ridiculous old fool was installed as president was precisely *because* he was so corrupt and compromised, and they knew they could control him, could make him do and say *anything*—even if no one can understand his garbled, senile blather.

There have been, to date, four suicides of January 6 defendants—four individuals whose lives felt hopeless to them because of the injustices they suffered from our corrupt DC judicial system, and the lengthy jail terms they faced for simply walking into a building, touching nothing, looking around, and walking back out. Matthew Perna, Mark Aungst, Christopher Stanton, and twenty-two-year-old Jord Meacham are all proof of the horrible human toll that these unjust prosecutions and disproportionate sentences have taken on this country. For them, and for the other victims I have met, been inspired by, and grown to love; for the families I have wept with; for Victoria White and Sarah McAbee; for Geri Perna; for Derek Kinnison and Tony Martinez, and for all the others, I will not stop trying to shine a light on one of the darkest chapters in our country's history. And I will continue to refute the huge lie the government continues to tell about January 6, 2021.

Capitol Punishment 2: The War on Truth will be released in early 2024.

⁙ CHAPTER 14 ⁙

RUSH LIMBAUGH AND ME

No book about my life would be complete without acknowledging what a huge part Rush Limbaugh played in it, and how his courage and perseverance inspired and informed me.

In 1990, I was living in North Carolina with my wife and newborn daughter, driving long distances for auditions, and trying to get my acting career started. Many of those trips were from western North Carolina to Wilmington, NC, a four-hundred-mile, six-and-a-half-hour drive one way. This was pre-cell phone, pre-internet, pre-SiriusXM, so there was nothing but the radio to keep you awake and alive. I would scan up and down the FM dial until I got tired of singing along, then switch over to AM, where it was mostly rural preachers and the odd trading-post-type show, people selling antiques or old appliances or cars, etc.

And then one day, I came upon this voice—this warm, jocular, joyful, sonorous, pleasant voice—bragging about his "talent on loan from God" and tying half his brain behind his back to make it fair to the callers—talking about politics, the news of the day, the silly things he'd read in the newspapers, playing funny song parodies—and he was making fun of *Democrats*. And at that time, this simply was not done.

And I thought, *Who the hell is this guy?*

For you young whipper-snappers out there, it's hard to understand what life was like before Rush. There was *no one*, and I mean no one, like him. There was no Fox News, no Sean Hannity, not really even a talk-radio format, not on the national level. Rush started it ALL. And the bond he built with his audience was based not on politics as much as it was humor. No one was funnier than Rush. He was fearless taking on the leftists.

Perhaps his greatest gift to us was how he modeled *courage* in the face of the most vociferous hate from horrified leftists that anyone could imagine. Because he upset their system. He screwed up the bullying game they had going. And he showed us all that it could be done, that the world could call you all the favorite names meant to silence you—racist, sexist, bigot, homophobe—and you could laugh at it and ridicule it, just like Rush did, and you would be fine.

He showed us all that the Left did not define him—or, by extension, us. And he talked to us like every single one of us was a dear friend—and in our hearts, we made friends with Rush.

It is nearly impossible for me to put into words how much Rush has meant to me over the years. Working in Hollywood among the leftists in power, I organized my day around Rush. If I had a commute, I tried to schedule it so that I would be in the car between noon and 3:00 p.m. EST so I could listen. I even bought a shortwave radio from Radio Shack (google that, kids) so I could hear Rush from anywhere on Earth, even if he was preempted by current events and the like. I was a Rush 24/7 member from the first moment it was possible to be one.

Because I was as a small-town kid pursuing the seemingly impossible goal of making a living as an actor, I saw myself in Rush. When he talked about wanting to be on the radio from a very young age, and knowing that radio was what he wanted to do with his life—when he talked about the jobs he'd been fired from, and all the setbacks he'd encountered along the way and how he had still persevered—he gave me *hope*. He made me believe, perhaps more than any other single person in my life besides my mom, that *I could do it* if I just kept going.

And so I did. Even after I got my acting career going, after I was lucky enough to land the pivotal bad-guy role in *Fried Green Tomatoes*, playing wife-beating Klansman Frank Bennett (the first of many Democrats I would play over my career), and after I'd moved to Los Angeles to continue to work, I continued to listen to Rush every day. He sustained me through all the disappointments and the triumphs, and helped me have a sense of humor about them. And most of all, he let me know that *I was not alone* in being a conservative, even while I was in the thick of the den of leftist thieves, bullies, and vipers that is Hollywood.

In 2010, I was cast as Art Mullen in the TV show *Justified*, a role that perhaps has become the signature role of my career. Rush said repeatedly on the air how much he liked the show, which thrilled me to no end. I was so proud that my friend Rush liked some of *my* work. Nothing made me feel like I had made it more than that fact.

And then, one day, it happened. Rush mentioned *me*, *by name*, on the air. My phone blew up with friends calling to tell me. I couldn't believe it! By then, Twitter had arrived on the scene, and I was already friends with Rush's brother David, so I immediately tweeted him. One thing led to another, and then, the next day, I got a call from Bo Snerdley *himself*, asking if I would like to come on the show and be interviewed by the Maha Rushie *himself*!

After that, I became completely insufferable. I bragged constantly that I had been on Rush's show longer than Dick Cheney, that Rush was a friend of mine, that I was the biggest international film and television star to ever appear on the Rush Limbaugh program, etc. The man with half his brain tied behind his back had taught me well.

And then my longtime one-sided friendship with Rush became a little bit mutual. Which, of course, was surreal.

I had the privilege of meeting Rush in person, of introducing him at a speech he gave to that top-secret Hollywood conservative group that has no name and in fact never existed. I even exchanged gifts with El Rushbo. A few times over the years, he would see a show I was in and write to me about it. It always seemed surreal to me when I would shoot him an email and he would answer it or read it on the air, or when Bo Snerdley would text me. It felt like a dream, like it couldn't be happening.

And toward the end of Rush's life, when he talked about how blessed he was to have lived the life he had, I saw myself in him again. There is no question that I have been a very fortunate fellow. I have been able to forge a living for myself and my beautiful family by acting, which is a miracle in and of itself. But still, the most incredible, preposterous thing that has ever happened to me occurred on December 27, 2017, when I had the honor of guest-hosting *The Rush Limbaugh Show.*

That was a gift to me in so many ways. I'm not a radio guy, but I was dragged across the finish line that day by the great Bo Snerdley and the amazing Mike Mimone, and it remains the single most surreal event in my life. It's an honor I still can't believe I received.

The day before I guest-hosted, Kraig Kitchin passed along a message to me from Rush. Rush had told him to ask me why I wanted to get into the radio business.

I told Kraig to tell Rush that I really wasn't sure if I did, but I knew that I just wanted to know what it felt like to *be Rush* for one day.

And it gave me even more of an appreciation of how great Rush was, when I experienced exactly how hard it is to be on the radio for three hours *just once*, let alone fifteen hours a week, fifty weeks a year, for thirty years, at the very top of the mountain, with no one else ever even close.

I have so many memories: laughing with him at his song parodies, crying with him when he had his painkiller issues, praying for him when his hearing went, and—of course—sobbing when he announced that he had the cancer that would ultimately end his life.

I heard from so many Rush fans after the announcement of his cancer diagnosis, sharing their concern, offering their prayers, and telling me how much Rush meant to them. I heard from a long-haul trucker, for whom Rush was the best part of his day, who had to pull his truck over a couple of times that day and cry.

> *Hey Nick. the news from Rush Limbaugh has hit me kinda hard. I grew up with him, starting in my dad's car, and I lost my dad in the fall of 2018. I'm just some dude who's listened to him since the early 90's, but I know you have a relationship with him. If you have the chance to talk to him personally, please let him know that I and my family are praying for him. he has generations who've listened to and learned from him…I guess it's that way with a lot of you famous folks.. we feel like we know you and we hurt when you do, even if we've never met.*

And when that sad day came, I was just like everyone else among in Rush's 30 million-plus audience. We grieved—not just because we agreed with his politics, not for the validation and courage he modeled for us, not just because we would miss hearing his inimitable take on the day's events. We grieved like he was part of our family—and he was. We grieved because we loved him, and we knew he loved us.

If it can ever be said about someone that he did not live in vain, that his life made a difference, that someone is Rush Limbaugh. He showed us the way. May we have the same courage that he had, to laugh in the face of hatred, to defend this country and what it stands for, and to do so with intelligence and humor—and love.

He loved us, his audience. We were family to him too.

God bless Rush Limbaugh, and God bless the United States of America.

TRANSCRIPT OF NICK SEARCY HOSTING
THE RUSH LIMBAUGH SHOW
DECEMBER 27, 2017

Let me explain the Trump phenomenon to you through the prism of one of my favorite art forms: professional wrestling.

Now for the eight years of Obama regime, many of us out here not only felt like the country was turning into a socialist hellhole, we didn't see anybody standing up to it. And we saw a lot of people in the GOP campaigning on, say, repealing Obamacare, or stopping the appointment of activist leftist judges, or opening up access to our natural resources (DRILL, BABY, DRILL)—but then when they're elected, they just get steamrolled by the Democrats.

This is where professional wrestling comes in. You're going to have to know a little bit about the history of it. For years, the GOP has been functioning like the old-fashioned good guy or the baby face wrestler. That's the terminology: "Baby Face." Remember that. The baby face would always get cheated by the "heels." And usually, they would lose. They'd get hit by the foreign object, or the masked bad guys would kick the hero in the head with a loaded boot, and Gorgeous George—it goes back that far—when Gorgeous George with his valet spraying perfume in the guy's eyes, and they would get pinned, one-two-three, and the crowd would be outraged—but the psychology of this, for the audience, was that the baby face was "playing fair," and they were losing with integrity. And that was the lesson for the audience.

How many times have you heard a Republican say things like, "We're better than that" or "We can't stoop to their level?"

Professional wrestling went on like that for years, because wrestling has always been about making the audience hate the bad guy. Wrestling fans are called "marks," and hating the bad guy is what makes a mark buy tickets. The heel's job is to make the audience so furious that they're willing to pay money to see somebody kick that guy's ass, or even pretend to kick his ass, and this went on for years—until Hulk Hogan came along. Hulk Hogan redefined the baby face role because he was the first wrestler who would pick up the foreign object, pick up the steel chair, and he would hit the heel back with it.

He started fighting like the heel fought. And the audience? They went crazy. They've been waiting for this for years. And this is why Hulk Hogan was the greatest wrestler on earth for a number of years. This is why WrestleMania came around. And it also spawned the "Attitude Era," probably the most profitable time in WWE history, where you really could not tell the difference between the heels and the faces—"Stone Cold" Steve Austin actually wrestled like a heel, and he became perhaps the most popular wrestler of all time

So, for years, the Democrats have had all these awful, absolutely despicable heels—like "Stretch" Pelosi and "Macho Man" Harry Reid and Chuck "Fake Tears" Schumer—and they constantly did dirty, underhanded things: throwing out the filibuster whenever it suits them or changing the Senate rules to ram the healthcare bill down our throats. This is what they do. They bend the rules to suit themselves whenever they have the votes to do it. They fight dirty.

So for years, when those of us in Rush's audience get tired of the Democrat heels cheating, and start roaring for the "Baby Face" GOP to hit back, the GOP would finally pick up the steel chair, or the brass knuckles or whatever—and then just put the steel chair down, spewing some drivel like, "We have to be better than that. We have to preserve the traditions of the Senate, and it would not be fair to our esteemed colleagues on the other side of the aisle."

And so the GOP would get pinned like that again and again, with the audience going home furious and empty. It happened with McCain, it happened with Romney. They refused to fight, and they became baby face jobbers for the heel Obama. They laid down and let themselves be pinned.

And then suddenly here comes this guy Trump, who comes into the arena swinging a steel chair! He's not even waiting for the heels to cheat! He's clocking everybody with the steel chair—the CNNs, the fake news, weak Republicans like "Low Energy" Jeb Bush, "Crooked" Hillary Clinton—he's laying everybody out in the arena, one after the other!

And that's why the crowd goes wild for Trump! Because—finally—they see someone FIGHTING BACK. And that is also why the Democrat heels absolutely hate Trump's guts—because he fights dirty, like they do.

CHAPTER 15

IF YOU SMELL-L-L-L WHAT NICK IS COOKING...

Anyone who really knows me knows that I have been a professional wrestling fan my whole life. I've watched it from the days of George Becker and Johnny Weaver tag-teaming against the Masked Infernos. I remember when Ric Flair debuted in Mid-Atlantic Championship Wrestling.

In high school, around 1975, a bunch of my friends and I went to the Asheville Civic Center one afternoon to watch Johnny Valentine and Wahoo McDaniel fight for the championship belt. They beat each other half to death, bled all over the arena, hit each other with everything they could find. Valentine won, I remember, with a sneaky little roll-up, and then had to be carried out of the arena because Wahoo had beaten him up so badly. After the match, we were standing out in the parking lot, jazzed up and excited about what we had seen, not wanting to go home, and we saw a van go by—and Wahoo was driving it, and Johnny Valentine was sitting in the passenger's seat beside him! And it dawned on me: This was a show! Professional wrestling was theater!

And I actually loved it even *more* after that. It became like a joke that I was in on. Watching the audience became part of the show. And I still love it, to this day.

For a long time, I thought I wanted to be a professional wrestler—as the great Dusty Rhodes said, "Deep down, EVERY southern boy wants to be a wrestler"—but once I figured out that it would mean a lot of weight lifting and rolling around with sweaty guys and falling down and getting hurt a lot, I decided to stick to doing plays.

When we were dating, Leslie told me she had never been to a wrestling match, I was appalled. I said, "This will not stand." One of our first dates was going to see Hulk Hogan wrestle in Madison Square Garden. I told her that she *had* to experience it at least once. We were both struggling actors at the time, having met in an off-Broadway play (which we performed one night for an audience of *one*), and I distinctly remember, during the Hogan match, while the sold-out arena was going wild, Leslie saying to me:

"Look at all these people! Can you imagine if all these people went to the theater?"

And I replied, "What? This is the *ultimate* theater! Protagonist versus antagonist! That's why all the people are here!"

One of the unexpected perks of being on *Justified* was that I finally got to realize my dream of being in a professional wrestling match. I had become friends with pro wrestler and fellow North Carolinian Matt Hardy of Hardy Boys fame, who was a fan of the show. At the time, Matt was wrestling on the indie circuit, taking a break from WWE, and I would make short YouTube videos from the set of *Justified*, cutting promos on Matt's opponents, which Matt would then post to drive up audience interest. I remember cutting one on a wrestler named Kevin Steen, who later became my favorite modern-day wrestler, "KO" Kevin Owens, talking to Matt about how hard it must be to wrestle Kevin, because the smell must be so bad. I distinctly remember Kevin writing me a DM on Twitter at the time, saying "Thanks for the heat!"

I also cut promos for Matt on the Briscoe Brothers, Jay and Mark, one of the greatest unsung tag teams I have ever seen. And then one day in 2014, Matt asked if I would like to come to Nashville and accompany him to ringside as his manager at the Ring of Honor *Best in the World* pay-per-view event. I jumped at the chance.

The match was a hardcore tag-team championship match, no DQ, anything goes, between the Brisco Brothers, Jay and Mark, and Matt and his partner, Mike Bennett, whose wife and manager was Maria Kanellis. I arrived at the arena that afternoon early, and we spent about an hour and a half in the ring, talking through the match.

In the promos I had done for Matt, I was a heel, bragging about what a big star I was in Hollywood, showing off my little Peabody Award trophy that I had received for being part of the cast of *Justified*, saying how stinky the chicken-farming Briscoes were, etc. So it was decided that at one point I would throw my Peabody into the ring to Matt, who would then hit one of the Briscoes with it and try to pin him. He would kick out, and then while everyone was down, I would crawl into the ring to retrieve my precious Peabody trophy. But Jay would pick up the trophy and refuse to give it to me. I would then yell, "Get your filthy hands off my precious

Peabody Award!" Then he would kick me in the stomach, smash me on my back, and I'd fall to the mat, and Mark would hit me with an elbow drop from the top rope, and they'd roll me out of the ring.

When they pitched all this to me, I said, "That sounds like it will be great and really funny, and the audience will love it. But that elbow off the top rope…won't that hurt?"

They all looked at me for a moment, and then Mark Briscoe said, "Well…you'll feel it. But it won't *hurt* you."

Then they set about teaching me how to protect myself when the elbow drop happened—hold my arms across my chest so that the impact lands mostly on the arms, sit up off the mat a little right when the blow comes, breathe out and "tense up" my muscles, brace for the impact, and so on. So I felt like I was going to be okay—even though we didn't practice it.

But of course, when the moment came, in front of two thousand fans, I forgot everything they told me. I executed the first part of the match perfectly. I came out with Matt Hardy in a full-length black coat, with sunglasses and a gold dollar-sign chain around my neck, holding up my Peabody Award, and taunting the crowd, screaming, "This award is for EXCELLENCE in TELEVISION! Something you LOSERS will never know anything about!" I got some good heat for that.

But when it came time for the big elbow off the top rope, I forgot everything. I did everything right up to that point— took the kick to the stomach, no injury, knocked down to the mat, no injury—but when I looked up from flat on my back and saw Mark Briscoe on the top rope launching himself into the air, I thought, *Holy shit, that guy's going to kill me!*

I involuntarily flinched, turned a little to the side, and Mark's flying elbow caught me right in the ribs. I rolled out of the ring and was carried to the back of the arena. My dream had come true.

But I hurt for six months. I think I must have cracked a rib or two. It hurt when I laughed, when I jogged—and I couldn't admit it to Leslie. For months before the match, she'd been telling me, "You're crazy. You had better not do this. You are going to get hurt." And I kept saying, "No, no. I'm going to be fine. I've been a fan all my life! I know what I'm doing!" So I just had to suck it up and pretend I was okay.

But I will never forget that experience, and I will always be grateful to Matt Hardy for making it happen for me. I got to be a heel wrestling manager in a professional show; I got to "take a bump," as they say; and I got to really feel that incredible adrenaline rush when two thousand people boo you, when what you are doing makes them *hate your guts.* I've always loved the heels, loved watching how they made the fans hate them, and I got to do it, just for one night, a night that I will never forget.

But that's enough. My professional wrestling career is over. I'm officially retired. I have nothing but mad respect for the men and women of professional wrestling. It's like acting while playing football without pads. I get my "heel persona" kicks on Twitter these days. Matt Hardy told me he explains my Twitter feed to his buddies by telling them, "Nick's playing a heel on Twitter."

And he's right. And I don't get my ribs hurt on Twitter.

Matt Hardy and Mike Bennett remain friends of mine to this day. My experience with the people I've met in the professional wrestling world is that they are some of the kindest, most generous, and most respectful people to their fans that I have ever met. When my dear wheelchair-bound nephew Todd, the biggest wrestling fan in the family besides me, was hospitalized early in 2023, all of my wrestling friends face-timed and/or called to lift his spirits—Matt and Jeff Hardy, Mike Bennett and Maria Kanellis, Eric Bischoff, and even Todd's favorite wrestler, Rhea Ripley. I'll never forget their kindnesses to Todd, and I will always cherish my brief time in the "Squared Circle."

In Memory of Jay Briscoe
(Jamin Dale Pugh)
1984-2023

▓ CHAPTER 16 ▓

GRATITUDE

I have had, and continue to have, such a blessed life and career.

As I bring this book to its conclusion, my big breaks are continuing. In 2021, I acted in two westerns back-to-back, both filmed in the same beautiful town of Livingston, Montana (thankfully, neither of them was with Alec Baldwin, so I'm here to tell the tale. Too soon? Sorry.)

The Old Way, starring the great Nicolas Cage and a talented young actress named Ryan Kiera Armstrong, marked the first time in my nearly thirty-year career that I actually got to ride a horse on camera, believe it or not. Working with Mr. Cage was a pleasure. He was always very prepared and ready to go, very generous, and very professional. I had a wonderful time with him, and I hope to work with him again. The film was directed by an old friend, Brett Donowho, who did a wonderful job with a very unique twist on a western—wherein both of the main characters were unable to feel emotion. I highly recommend it, if you haven't seen it.

Right after that, I returned to Livingston to play the title role in the Daily Wire's production of *Terror on the Prairie*. I played the captain of a band of outlaws terrorizing the great Gina Carano out on the plains of 1875 Montana. It was one of the best roles I have had, spewing Bible verses as I cut throats and murdered all the men I could find who were responsible for the death of my daughter ten years earlier. *Terror* is a classic revenge western, with great performances by Gina, Cowboy Cerrone, Tyler Fischer and the late Heath Freeman. My only regret about the film is that it was not seen by more people, as it was only available to Daily Wire subscribers—and to this day, over a year after its release, is only on the Daily Wire website. Hopefully, in the future, the Daily Wire will find a way to make *Terror* easier to access, as I believe it is important for films made by conservative outlets to be part of the mainstream, available to everyone.

(A side note: One day during the filming of *Terror*, we got the horrible news of the deadly accident on the set of Alec Baldwin's film *Rust*. This, of course, shook everyone up a little, since we were firing an awful lot of weapons in our movie as well. We were already a very safety-conscious set, but the incident brought home the fact that the gun safety protocols that were in place had to be followed to perfection to make sure no one was hurt or injured. Coincidentally, it was reported that for the armorer on *Rust*, Hannah Guttierez-Reed, this was only her second feature film as lead armorer. Her first job as lead armorer was —you guessed it—*The Old Way*.)

So, in spite of my politics—and frankly, sometimes because of them—I continue to work in the entertainment industry, as an actor as well as a producer/director and even as a writer. At this moment, in the last quarter of 2023, I have two feature films that have just been released (*Muzzle* and

Police State), another one (*Reagan*) set for release in 2024, and a Netflix miniseries (*The Perfect Couple*), to be released whenever the strike ends and we are able to finish it.

I also have cowritten two feature screenplays with Blake Ellis, the actor who worked with me in the Laguna Playhouse production of Mike Bencivenga's *Billy and Ray*, that I also plan to direct: *Infiltration*, an action movie set on the US border, and *Where I'm Bound*, a drama set in the world of gospel quartet music in the '60s. Both are in the process of being funded by two different companies. Blake and I had so much fun pretending to be Raymond Chandler and Billy Wilder writing a screenplay together, that we decided to write screenplays together in real life!

As a guest columnist, I have written op-ed pieces for RedState.com, Breitbart.com, and even one for the once prestigious *National Review*, before it collapsed completely into controlled opposition. I even got a chance to try my hand at stand-up comedy, thanks to an invitation from the great Rodney Carrington to go out with him and do a few minutes as an opener during the height of the COVID nonsense. Rodney did a few dates during that time in states that were open, like Florida and Arizona, and was playing comedy clubs again, since the larger venues he usually plays were closed. I went out with him for about a year off and on, as a fill in when his usual opener was unavailable.

I could write another entire book about my comedy career experiences. Suffice to say that I was utterly terrified when it started, but by the end, I had opened for Rodney a few times when the big arenas reopened, doing up to twenty minutes in front of fifteen hundred to two thousand people!

It was exhilarating, and I will always be grateful to Rodney for giving me the chance to try it. Again, like my experience with professional wrestling, it gave me true insight into, and a tremendous respect for, the stand-up comedy profession.

Of course, most of my best jokes were funny things my wife, Leslie, said, because, as Jon Avnet realized during *Justified*, she is the true talent in our family. For example, probably my best joke was this true story: After *Fried Green Tomatoes*, in which I played a wife-beating husband, I got a lot of offers to play wife beaters, rapists, sexual harassers, etc. (Punchline: I mean let's face it, I've played a lot of Democrats), and I said to Leslie, "Why do you think I keep getting offers to play men who beat up women?" And Leslie said, "Well, you don't look like you can beat up a man."

Since then, I have opened for a few more comic friends of mine—Tyler Fischer and Chrissie Mayr, among others—and it's a wonderful skill to have in my pocket. I am not a headliner, but I've got a solid ten to twelve minutes. But since I'm not going to be funnier than the headliner, I'm a perfect opening act.

So nothing has slowed down for me. If anything, things have accelerated. I continue to be contacted about new projects and possibilities all the time. And perhaps the question I am most often asked is: How do you continue to work? How have you not been canceled yet?

The short answer is: I don't know. For example, I don't know why God led me to be at the US Capitol on January 6, 2021—but I know that He did. I also don't know why God protected me while I was there and led me to places where I would not be in danger of committing any infraction that might have landed me in legal trouble (although, granted, it could happen to me at any moment, since our government is continuing to persecute innocent Americans who did nothing wrong). In meeting and talking to so many J6ers, and hearing their stories of where they were that day, what they did, how they were swept into the tunnel or the building by the sheer thrust of the crowd, or how they witnessed women being attacked by police and felt called to do something, I often wonder, *Why me, Lord? Why was I protected from being in those places?*

Had I been in their position, had I seen what they saw, I probably would have done exactly what they did. And I would be in the DC jails, held without bond and without trial for years, facing a corrupt judge and an utterly partisan jury, without a prayer of getting a fair verdict, no matter how well I was defended—another political prisoner in what is supposedly the freest country on the face of the Earth.

There but for the grace of God go I, indeed.

I don't know why I have been, and continue to be, so blessed, both in my personal life and in my professional life, when I have taken stances that are so unpopular in Hollywood. I can only conclude that, for whatever His reasons, God has placed me where he wants me to be, and I am there to do His will. And I feel like the least I can do is be grateful.

I am grateful for the career that I have enjoyed, the family that God has blessed me with, the friends that I have enjoyed for many years, as well as the new friends I have made that have changed my life—friends who have opened new doors for me—doors, in many cases, that I did not know were there.

But most of all, I am grateful that God has given me the ability to see through the manipulations and the evil that is daily being advanced in America and throughout the world.

So many of the people in my industry, in Hollywood, are so blind, so incapable of perceiving basic, obvious truth, so devoid of common sense, and so invested in the moral superiority that has been inculcated into them by the media, that they may never find the real truth until it is too late. And I pray for them every day.

I thank God for the parents that raised me; the wife, Leslie, that God gave me; the amazing, beautiful children, Chloe and Omar, that He blessed me with; my brilliant sister Mitzi; and the rich tapestry of friends that I have accumulated over the years. And, perhaps most of all, the wisdom and discernment that following Him and His word have granted me, so that I am NOT susceptible to the barrage of brainwashing that has destroyed this country and brought us to the absolute brink of totalitarian, Orwellian, irreversible tyranny.

It gives me joy in times of despair that, even if all my efforts change nothing, even if everything I have done and continue to try to do has no effect, at least my eyes have been opened and I have been blessed with clarity of sight. And that does not come from my own wisdom. That blessing comes from God.

I look at it this way: If you are canceled by the mob, they silence you. But if you silence yourself because you are afraid of being canceled, they *still* silence you. So I encourage all of you out there, especially those of you in the creative arts to live without fear and boldly be yourself. Fearlessness is the greatest tool we have in fending off the Left's plans for this country. If anything can be gleaned from looking at my life and modestly successful career, I hope it is that I stood up for what I believed, and I gained far more than I lost.

I thank you, dear reader, for reading this book and for caring about my journey. That is another blessing to me, one that I don't deserve, and can never repay.

Jesus has been with me for my entire life—even during the times when I was not with Him, He was with me.

And I am so grateful. I try to practice gratitude every day of my life.

I highly recommend it.

NICK SEARCY FILMOGRAPHY

2024-TO BE RELEASED
Reagan
The Perfect Couple (series)
Capitol Punishment 2 (producer)

2023
Shadow Brother Sunday (short)
The Warrant: Breaker's Law
The Old Way
Muzzle
Police State

2022
Terror on the Prairie

2021
Capitol Punishment (also producer)
Hotel Coppelia
The Man from Nowhere

2020
America, America, God Shed His Grace on Thee
    (also producer)
Manhunt: Deadly Games (miniseries)

2019

Unbelievable (miniseries)
The Hot Zone (miniseries)
9–1–1
The Best of Enemies

2018

The Ranch
Gosnell: The Trial of America's Biggest Serial Killer (director)
Lethal Weapon
Hunter
Destined to Ride
Legal Action
Chicago Med

2017

The Shape of Water
Three Billboards Outside Ebbing, Missouri
Landline

2016

Zoobiquity
Greater
The Sweet Life
11.22.63

2015

Try Hard: The Rex Derby Story
Key & Peele
Justified (series; 6 seasons)
Hot in Cleveland

2014

Locker 212
Hawaii Five-0
The Dollanganger Saga
Intelligence
New Partner

2013

Mom
NTSF:SD:SUV
Archer
Metamorphosis (short)

2012

Chloe + Zoë (web series)
Gone

2011

Moneyball
Svetlana

2010

The Mentalist
The Last Song
Blood Done Sign My Name

2009

Lie to Me
Easy Money (series; 1 season)
The Ugly Truth
Cold Storage
Without a Trace

2008

XII

Boston Legal

2007

Criminal Minds

The Comebacks

Welcome to Paradise

NCIS

Timber Falls

Army Wives

An American Crime

2006

The Dead Girl

Flicka

CSI: Crime Scene Investigation

2005

Mall Cop

Rodney (series; 2 seasons)

Deadly End

2004

The Lost Cause

The Assassination of Richard Nixon

The Last Summer

Capital City

2003

Line of Fire
The West Wing
Runaway Jury
The Guardian
Lucky
Head of State
CSI: Miami

2002

The Angel Doll
Double Teamed
One Hour Photo

2001

Seven Days (series; 3 seasons)

2000

Cast Away
Tigerland

1999

CI5: The New Professionals

1998

About Sarah
From the Earth to the Moon (series)

1997

Carolina Low (director)
Chicago Hope

Early Edition
Perfect Crime

1996

A Step Toward Tomorrow
Nash Bridges
American Gothic (series, 1 season)

1995

Stolen Innocence
Naomi & Wynonna: Love Can Build a Bridge
Double Rush

1994

Desert Winds
Nell
The War
Roswell
Thunder Alley
In the Best of Families

1993

Return to Lonesome Dove
The Real McCoy
The Fugitive
Deadly Relations
When Love Kills: The Seduction of John Hearn
Losers in Love
House of Cards
Love Field

1992

In the Heat of the Night
A Mother's Right: The Elizabeth Morgan Story
I'll Fly Away
L.A. Law
Black Magic

1991

Fried Green Tomatoes
The Prince of Tides
Nightmare in Columbia County
Wife, Mother, Murderer
White Lie

1990

Days of Thunder
Unspeakable Acts

1985

Killin' Time (short)

ACKNOWLEDGMENTS

This book would not have existed had Johnny Russo not come to me with the crazy idea that someone might be interested in publishing a book about my career.

To my beautiful wife Leslie, who has helped me with auditions, inspired me, counseled me, comforted me, confronted me when necessary, and stuck with me, through thick and thin, for better and for worse, and made me laugh along the way, I pray I have been as good for you as you have been for me.

To my friends Andy and Blake and Mark who suffered through early drafts and told me what was missing;

To my beautiful children, Chloe and Omar, who continue to delight and inspire me with all they are creating and becoming;

And to my Mom and Dad, who gave me the freedom and the courage to become what I wanted to become,

This book is for all of you.